SANDRA BETZINA
SEWS FOR YOUR HOME

SANDRA BETZINA
SEWS FOR YOUR HOME

Sandra Betzina
and Debbie Valentine

The Taunton Press

The Taunton Press
Inspiration for hands-on living™

The Taunton Press, Inc., 63 South Main Street, PO Box 5506, Newtown, CT 06470-5506
e-mail: tp@taunton.com

Distributed by Publishers Group West

COVER DESIGN: Cathy Cassidy

INTERIOR DESIGN: Susan Fazekas

LAYOUT: Susan Fazekas

ILLUSTRATOR: Christine Erikson

PHOTOGRAPHER: Jack Deutsch

LIBRARY OF CONGRESS CATALOGING-IN-PUBLICATION DATA

Betzina, Sandra.
    Sandra Betzina sews for your home / Sandra Betzina and Debbie Valentine.
        p. cm.
    ISBN 1-56158-446-0
    1. Household linens. 2. Machine sewing. I. Valentine, Debbie. II. Title.
    TT387 .B48 2002
    646.2'1--dc21   20002003395

Printed in Malaysia
10 9 8 7 6 5 4 3 2 1

To my coauthor Debbie Valentine, for her ability to convert me—
a dedicated garment sewer—to the exciting and far easier world
of home-dec sewing through her vast knowledge, flexibility,
sense of humor, and incredible work ethic.

—SANDRA BETZINA

To my wonderful daughter, Tina, who will
someday, I hope, find her own Sandra Betzina.

—DEBBIE VALENTINE

ACKNOWLEDGMENTS

With Special Thanks

We would like to take this opportunity to thank Louise Canezari, Candie Frankel, Francesca Giacalone, and Kimberly Lang, all of whom helped us with their technical expertise and advice. Special thanks goes to Teresa Jepson, Edna and Don Wilson, and especially David Valentine for his time, tools, great attitude, and endless patience. For fabric donations, we are grateful to Calico Corners, Carol's Zoo, Poppy Fabric, Thai Silks, Down Etc., and Creator's Foam Shop.

Contents

INTRODUCTION

Making items for your home can be more satisfying than any sewing you have ever done. It's your chance to infuse your personality and creative ideas into the objects you see and use everyday, and you'll save a bundle of money in the process. Whether you are outfitting your first apartment or downsizing after the children have left home, it's easy to make your surroundings reflect your personality, needs, and tastes.

If you are used to sewing garments, you will find home-dec sewing much less demanding. It's a lot easier to fit a chair that, unlike a human body, doesn't gain or lose weight or worry about whether it looks slim enough! You're also likely to use a color palette that's different from the one you'd choose for your personal

wardrobe. You can spend money on fabric guilt-free, because the whole family will enjoy the finished product.

If you are a new sewer, home-dec items are a great place to begin because the fabrics are easy to work with and you don't have to fuss with the fit. The sewing skills needed are minimal—basically, just the ability to operate a sewing machine. You get instant gratification and compliments because the projects are big enough to be noticed.

The projects in this book are grouped into seven chapters geared to the various needs, people, and events that make up daily life. Some of the projects were inspired by items found in upscale stores, and others are practical, fun ideas we dreamed up on our own. Included are projects for children, gift items, big home-dec statements like draperies, and small accent pieces such as a neck roll.

Sidebars provide a wealth of information on a variety of topics, from how to buy a quality down comforter to using a blindstitch foot. You will get tips on sewing faux fur, velour, vinyl, sheer fabrics, and many others. Turn to the "Trick of the Trade" and "Scraps of Knowledge" boxes when you need to know more about techniques like making single- and double-welt cord and putting in zippers. Work-sheets are included to help you take measurements and figure out yardages for your projects. In short, here's your opportunity to work on a wide variety of projects while learning a multitude of skills.

In addition to the sewing, marking, and measuring tools already in your sewing room, you will need a carpenter's level, a T-square, a glue gun, and a staple gun. If you are planning to do a lot of home decorating, treat yourself to an electric staple gun, an investment that you will never regret. Your shopping expeditions will take you to new places: foam shops, websites that sell pillow forms in all sizes and shapes, and stores that specialize in home-dec fabrics. You will find full information on the products we used and where to find them in the Resources section on p. 198.

Start your adventure by flipping through the pages and marking the projects you want to make now. Put the faux-fur throw (p. 76) high on your list so that you can wrap yourself up in it for afternoon naps, even if you only have timc for one nap a week. Now, take a stroll around your house or apartment with a notepad in hand. Look at your surroundings with a critical eye. Where do you need window treatments? What areas could use a shot of color? What pieces of furniture should be re-covered? Don't rush. Enjoy the journey. Decide what you want to make, shop for the fabric and trim that will make it special, and spend some wonderful hours, working step by step, to bring your project to its thrilling completion.

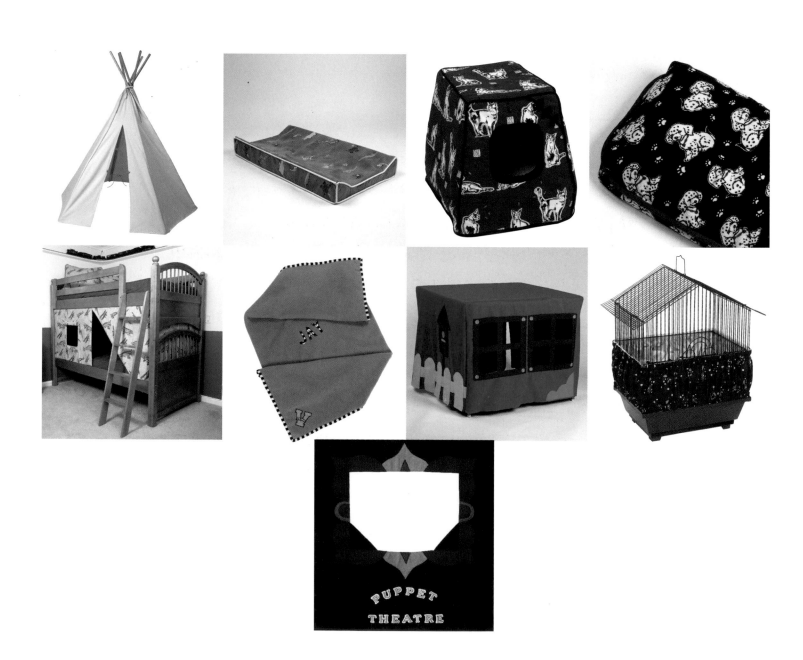

Part 1

KIDS AND PETS

This opening chapter involves making projects for those you love. You will have a lot of fun, whether your household includes children, pets, or both. For babies, there's a cuddly fleece blanket and a practical vinyl-covered changing pad. For children, there are several different projects that offer secret hideaways. How about a child's felt playhouse that slips on and off a folding card table? The puppet theater and bunk-bed fort were favorites of Sandra's children and have been immortalized in the family photo album with lots of memories to accompany them. If you own a cat, there's the litter box cover that blends in with the overall decor instead of screaming "litter box" the moment you enter the room. You'll also find items for the pet birds and puppies in your life. Let's start sewing!

Baby Blanket

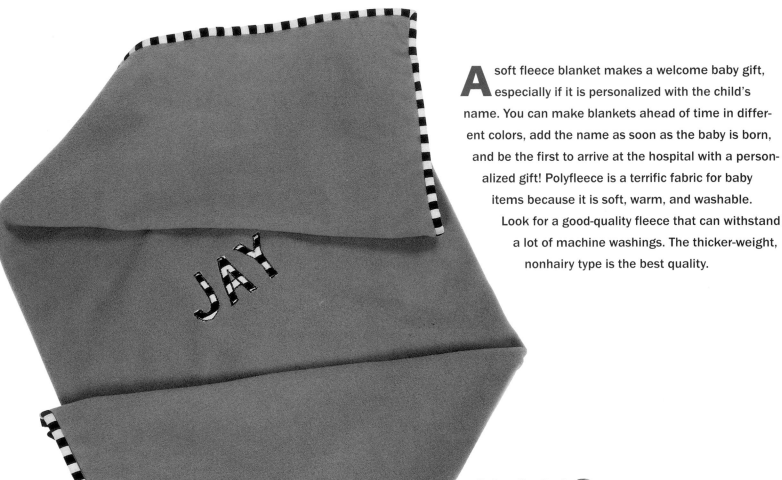

A soft fleece blanket makes a welcome baby gift, especially if it is personalized with the child's name. You can make blankets ahead of time in different colors, add the name as soon as the baby is born, and be the first to arrive at the hospital with a personalized gift! Polyfleece is a terrific fabric for baby items because it is soft, warm, and washable. Look for a good-quality fleece that can withstand a lot of machine washings. The thicker-weight, nonhairy type is the best quality.

A polyfleece blanket edged in knit fabric couldn't be softer for baby—or easier to sew for you.

Before You Begin see **Single Welt** on page 13.

FOR ONE 45-INCH-SQUARE BABY BLANKET, YOU'LL NEED:

- 1¼ yards polyfleece
- ½ yard cotton knit for binding
- Purchased letter appliqués, or fusible interfacing and 3-inch sign-lettering stencils (available at hardware and art supply stores)
- Solvy™ stabilizer
- Sulky® KK 2000 Temporary Spray Adhesive
- Measuring and marking tools
- General sewing/craft supplies

MAKING THE BLANKET

1 Preshrink the knit fabric in the washer and dryer. Failure to do so will cause the binding to draw up and pucker the first time the blanket is laundered. It is not necessary to preshrink polyfleece.

2 Trim 15 inches off the polyfleece to make a 45-inch square. (Save the scrap for another project.)

3 Cut the knit fabric across the grain, from selvage to selvage, making four or five 3½-inch-wide strips. Join the strips together end to end, until the strip is long enough to go around the fleece square. Press the binding in half lengthwise, wrong side in, to make a strip 1¾ inches wide.

DESIGN IDEA A striped knit makes binding that's fun to work with because it produces a checked edge effortlessly. Cut the strips perpendicular to the stripes, making sure the knit stretches in that direction. Sew the seams so that the stripe pattern continues uninterrupted.

4 Decide which side of the fleece you would prefer as the right side. Lay the fleece square right side up. Pin the knit binding strip to the fleece, raw edges matching. Start at the middle of the fleece edge, and leave a 4-inch tail. Stop pinning when you reach the first corner.

5 To prevent stretching, use a Teflon® foot or a walking foot. Machine-stitch the binding to the fleece with a scant ⅜-inch seam, no wider. Stop sewing ⅜ inch from the corner. Take the work out of the machine. Insert a pin in the binding even with the blanket edge.

6 Swing the pinned section up and to the left, even with the edge just sewn. At the same time, swivel the raw edge of the binding down, even with the new fleece edge.

7 Put the work back into the machine. Starting ⅜ inch from the corner, resume sewing. Continue stitching all around, turning the corners as you come to them, until you are 4 inches from the starting point.

8 Take the work out of the machine. Hand-walk the two ends of the binding together, and make a ¼-inch clip in the raw edges where you think they will join. Place the two strip ends right sides together, aligning the clips. Sew the ends together ¹⁄₁₆ inch in from the clips so that the seam will lie flat. Trim the seam allowance to ⅛ inch to eliminate bulk. Finish sewing the binding to the blanket edge.

9 Fold the binding to the wrong side of the fleece, enclosing the seam allowance. On the right side, pin along the seam well through all layers. Check the pinning from the wrong side to make sure the binding is at least ⅛ inch beyond the stitching line and secured all around.

STEP 9

10 Make a small tuck in each corner on the wrong side. Turn the work right side up. Machine-stitch in the seam well all around, catching the binding on the back of the blanket as you go.

STEP 10

APPLIQUÉING THE BLANKET

1 Use purchased or handmade letter appliqués to finish the blanket. To make your own appliqués, use professional sign-lettering stencils. Apply fusible interfacing to the wrong side of your letter fabric. Use the stencils to mark the desired letters on the interfacing, reversing nonsymmetrical letters and simplifying the lines for smoother sewing. Cut out the letters.

STEP 1

2 Lay the blanket right side up on a flat surface. Use pins to mark a baseline for the lettering at the center of the blanket or at a corner. Apply a light coat of spray adhesive to the wrong side of the appliqués, just enough to prevent them from shifting as you sew. Position the appliqués on the blanket and remove the pins.

3 Thread the machine so that the top thread matches the appliqué and the bobbin thread matches the fleece. Set the machine for a 3.0mm zigzag width and a 1.0mm (or shorter) stitch length. Slip a Solvy stabilizer sheet under the fleece to prevent stretching as you sew. Zigzag around each appliqué, letting the stitch fall on and off the edge. Tear away the stabilizer sheet. If the letters or the binding look a bit puffy after sewing, steam-press through a press cloth.

[WORKROOM TIP] Those little balls that form on the surface of fleece are caused by abrasion. To prevent excessive pilling, wash and dry polyfleece articles alone or with other fleece items on a gentle cycle.

Baby Changing Pad

If you have a new baby, you will be spending a lot of time changing diapers. Why not make the changing pad fun to look at and coordinated with the baby's room? A plain white vinyl pad can easily be covered with brightly colored or printed vinyl.

A soft vinyl covering looks good and stands up to lots of diaper changes.

FOR ONE CHANGING PAD, YOU'LL NEED:

- Simmons® Juvenile Products changing pad (available at baby stores and Toys "R" Us)
- 1½ yards vinyl
- ½ yard fabric for bottom of pad
- ¼ yard contrasting fabric for welt
- 7 yards ¼-inch-diameter welt cord
- Small needle-nose pliers
- Roller or Teflon presser foot
- Measuring and marking tools
- General sewing/craft supplies

CUTTING THE PIECES

1 Stand the changing pad on end on brown paper or newspaper, and trace the angled outline. Add ½ inch all around for the seam allowance. Even up the edges. Cut out the pattern on the outside line. Fold and retrim as needed to make the pattern symmetrical where required.

2 Cut the following pieces from vinyl: one 19-inch by 34½-inch piece for the top, two 5-inch by 34½-inch pieces for the sides, and two ends, using the pattern made in step 1.

3 Cut an additional 19-inch by 34½-inch piece from fabric for the bottom of the pad. This fabric will not be visible when the pad is in use, so use anything you want.

ASSEMBLING THE COVER

1 Use the welt cord and contrasting fabric to make 7 yards of covered single welt. The lip should be ½ inch wide.

DESIGN IDEA The welt can be covered with soft vinyl instead of fabric, but experiment first. Some vinyl is too thick and stiff to make a welt that will turn nicely in curved seams.

2 Sew the welt around each end piece of the changing pad, butting and joining the ends when you reach the starting point. Clip into the lip to turn the sharp corners.

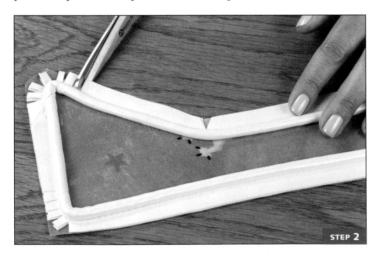

STEP 2

WORKROOM TIP Welted corners are always slightly rounded because of the excess bulk. Sew the welt as usual, stopping about 2 inches from the corner with the needle in the down position. Estimate where the corner will fall on the welt, and clip into the lip at this location three or four times, close to the stitching line, to enable the lip to lie as flat as possible. Continue sewing, easing the stitching around the corner.

3 Sew the remaining welt to the two long edges of each side piece of the changing pad. Use needle-nose pliers to pull out ⅜ inch of cord at one end. Clip off this bit of cord with scissors, and then let the remainder disappear back inside the welt covering. Do this at all four corners to reduce bulk.

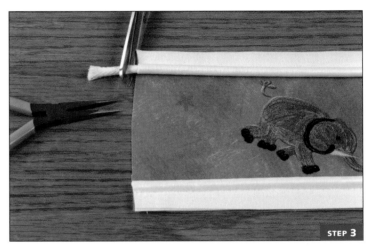

STEP 3

WORKROOM TIP Use a roller or Teflon foot on your machine when sewing vinyl. Increase the stitch length so that the vinyl seams will not be weakened by too much thread. Practice stitching on scraps of vinyl.

4 Sew the side and end pieces right sides together to form the outside rim. On each seam, start and stop the stitching ½ inch in from the edge. The unsewn ½ inch at each corner will provide ease to turn the corners without clipping.

5 Use paper clips to "pin" the vinyl top to the rim, right sides together, matching the edges all around. On the end pieces, clip in at each inside angle. Machine-stitch all around.

6 Pin the fabric bottom to the other edge of the rim, right sides together. Start at the middle of one short end and sew halfway around. Turn right side out. Insert the foam pad. Hand-sew the opening closed.

TRICK of the TRADE

SINGLE WELT

Welt is used to accentuate seams and give them a decorative, professional finish. It's made by enclosing a cord in a strip of fabric. The best-quality welt cord for home-dec use is from Conso®, a large company that makes many of the braids and fringes used in workrooms. The most popular size is ¼ inch diameter, but sizes up to 1 inch in diameter are available should you wish to make more of a statement. This flexible cord looks like thick cotton batting enclosed in a thread mesh tube. It does not have to be preshrunk.

The fabric strips to cover the cord can be cut on the bias or across the grain, depending on your final application. Bias strips give a nicer appearance on curved edges, such as scallops, and look especially attractive when cut from plaids or stripes. You'll need about ½ yard of 54-inch-wide fabric to make 2½ yards of bias-cut welt for a ¼-inch-diameter cord. Here's how to cover a cord of any diameter:

1 Determine the strip width by wrapping a tape measure around the cord. Let the tape extend ½ inch on either side for the seam allowance, and add an extra ⅛ inch for ease. A 1⅛-inch-wide strip covers a ¼-inch-diameter cord nicely.

2 Cut enough strips to cover the welt cord. Cut both ends of each strip at a 45-degree angle, and then sew the strips

together on the diagonal, to make one long continuous strip. The offset seams that result will reduce the bulk once the cord is enclosed.

3 Center the cord on the wrong side of the fabric strip, and bring the raw edges together, enclosing the cord inside. It is not necessary to pin the edges together, as long as the cord remains centered. Using a zipper foot, machine-baste close to the cord. Don't sew super close yet; you'll be doing that later. Be careful not to stretch the bias strip as you sew. The excess fabric to the right of the stitching is called the lip. The lip, measured from stitching line to raw edge, should be the same as the seam allowance for your project.

4 To join the welt to the project fabric, such as a pillow front, start in the middle of a straight edge, rather than at a corner. Place the welt on the right side of the project fabric, raw edges matching. With a zipper foot, begin stitching 1½ inches from the end of the welt, as close to the cord as possible. Stitch all around, stopping about 2 inches from the starting point. Back-tack to lock the stitches in place, and take the work out of the machine. Cut the covered cord 3 inches beyond the back tack, and pick out the welt stitching in this section to

expose the cord. Clip the exposed cord so that the ends can be butted together.

5 Tape or hand-sew the two cord ends together so that they do not come apart with use. First-aid tape is soft and flexible, but if the item will be laundered, hand stitching is more durable. Fold the loose fabric strip diagonally, wrong side in. Wrap it around the butted cords, matching the outer raw edges. Stitch down this last section with a zipper foot.

6 To complete a welted seam, place the two pieces of fabric—one with welt and one without—right sides together and edges matching. Stitch on the existing stitching line with a zipper foot to join the pieces together, enclosing the welt in the seam as you go.

Child's Tepee

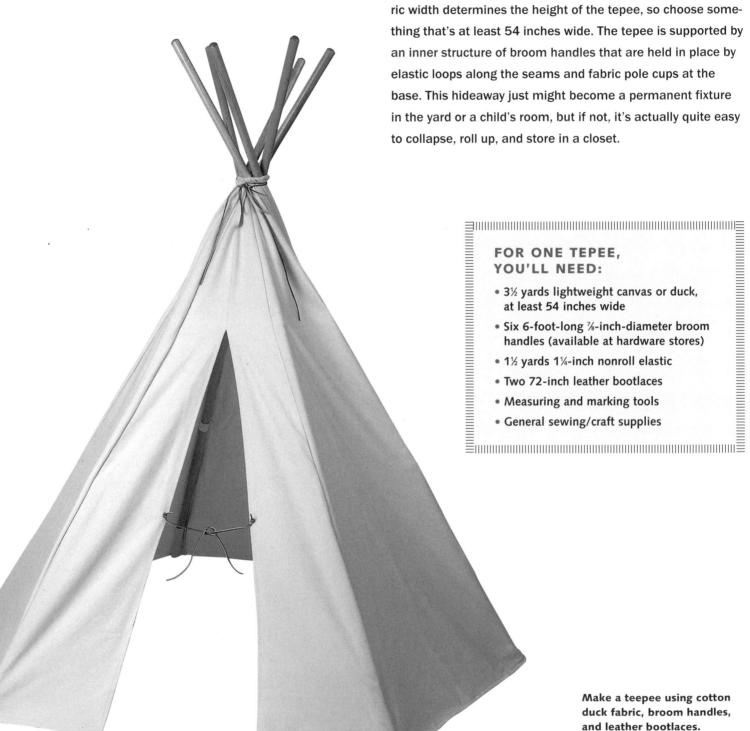

Maybe children don't play cowboys and Indians the way they used to, but this tepee is still a lot of fun. The fabric width determines the height of the tepee, so choose something that's at least 54 inches wide. The tepee is supported by an inner structure of broom handles that are held in place by elastic loops along the seams and fabric pole cups at the base. This hideaway just might become a permanent fixture in the yard or a child's room, but if not, it's actually quite easy to collapse, roll up, and store in a closet.

FOR ONE TEPEE, YOU'LL NEED:

- 3½ yards lightweight canvas or duck, at least 54 inches wide
- Six 6-foot-long ⅞-inch-diameter broom handles (available at hardware stores)
- 1½ yards 1¼-inch nonroll elastic
- Two 72-inch leather bootlaces
- Measuring and marking tools
- General sewing/craft supplies

Make a teepee using cotton duck fabric, broom handles, and leather bootlaces.

CUTTING THE FABRIC

1 Tape a few sheets of newspaper together to make a piece 54 inches long (or to match your fabric width) and at least 30 inches wide.

2 Fold the paper in half lengthwise. Measure out 2 inches from the fold on one edge and 15 inches from the fold on the other edge. Draw an angled line connecting these two points. Cut on the marked line through both layers. Open up the paper. The pattern should be a triangular shape measuring 30 inches across the base and 4 inches across the top.

3 Lay the fabric on a flat surface. Place the pattern on top, aligning the 30-inch and 4-inch edges on the selvages. Trace the outside edges. Rotate the pattern to mark the next piece, fitting the edges as closely as possible. Repeat to mark six tepee panels.

4 Cut out the panels. Fold one panel in half lengthwise and cut down the fold to make the front opening. Label these straight-cut edges with masking tape to indicate the tepee opening.

MAKING THE TEPEE

1 Serge or overcast the long edges, including the openings, of each panel. Sew the five full panels right sides together with a ½-inch seam allowance. Stitch from the top down, being careful not to stretch the seams as you sew. Add the two panels for the front opening last, being sure to keep the straight edges open. Press all the seams to one side. Serge, overcast, or narrow-hem the top and bottom edges.

2 Cut twelve 4-inch-long pieces of elastic. Bring the short ends of each piece together, and stitch to form a loop. Lay the tent facedown. Pin two elastic loops to each seam and each side of the front opening, 16 inches and 34 inches from the narrow top edge. Stitch in place. The loops will be used to secure the poles.

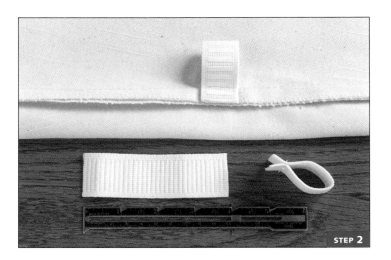

3 For the pole cups, cut six 4½-inch by 6½-inch pieces from the leftover fabric. Fold each piece in half lengthwise, right side out, and sew the side and one end together with a ½-inch seam allowance. Sew a pole-cup seam to each tepee seam 1 inch above the lower edge.

DESIGN IDEA Let the children get involved with fabric paints and stencils to decorate the tepee and bring it to the next level. The best time to paint the tepee is after the seams are sewn but before the seam above the doorway is closed up. You can lay the tepee flat so that it is a ready canvas for their artwork. Feathers and beads make nice additions near the top.

4 To make the opening, align the straight-cut edges right sides together. Beginning 6 inches from the top, back-tack, sew forward for 10 inches, and back-tack again. Press the seam open. Press the free edges ½ inch to the wrong side and topstitch.

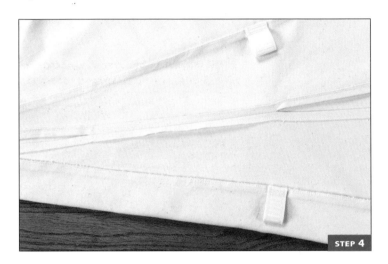

STEP 4

5 Cut two 12-inch lengths of leather bootlace. Join one end · of each lace to the tepee opening 22 inches above the lower edge.

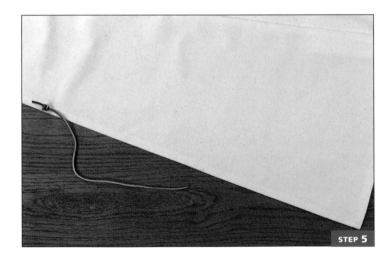

STEP 5

6 Press the top edge of the tepee ½ inch to the wrong side. Stitch to form a casing. Thread a 72-inch leather bootlace through the casing, allowing the extra to hang out at each end.

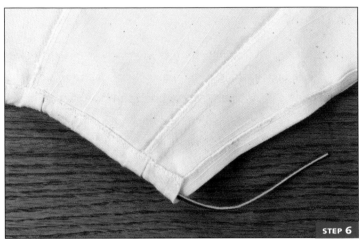

STEP 6

7 To set up the tepee, turn it right side out. Begin feeding the poles one at a time into the top opening, through the elastic loops, until the end lodges in its pole cup. When all the poles are inserted, gather the ends together at the top. Pull the leather tie tightly around them, wrapping twice and then tying in a bow for easy dismantling later. Spread out the poles as far as possible at the base.

Child's Playhouse

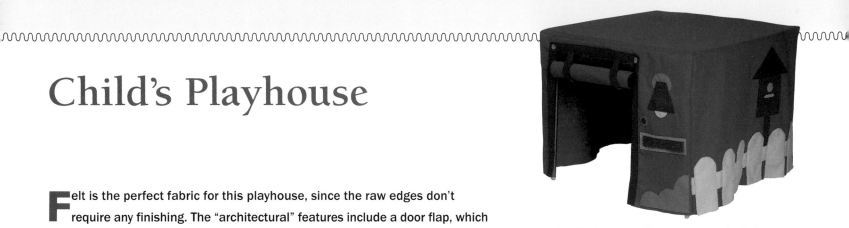

Felt is the perfect fabric for this playhouse, since the raw edges don't require any finishing. The "architectural" features include a door flap, which is held open with tabs and Velcro hook-and-loop tape, and a double window on the rear wall. Let the children help you out with other embellishments, or page through an upscale catalog of toys or children's clothing for motif ideas. The card-table support doesn't have to be in tiptop condition, as long as it's sturdy.

A felt playhouse fits over a standard-size folding card table, making it extra easy to disassemble and store.

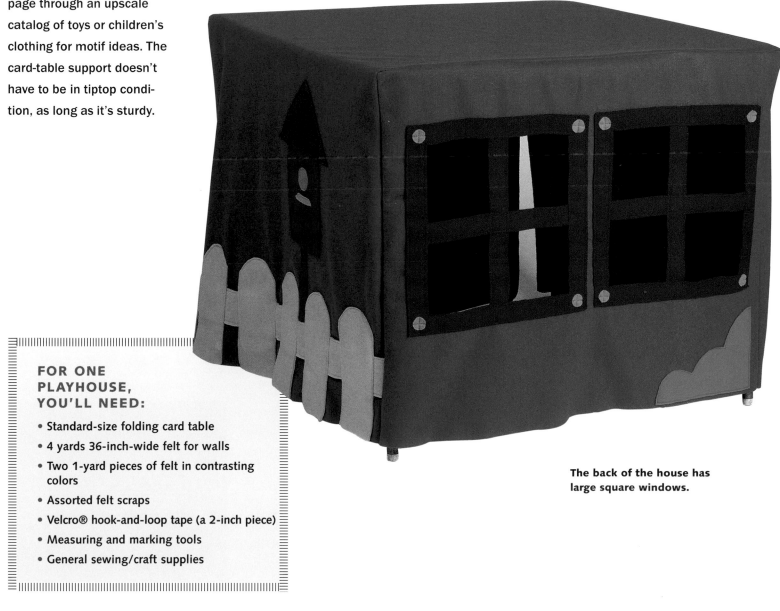

FOR ONE PLAYHOUSE, YOU'LL NEED:

- Standard-size folding card table
- 4 yards 36-inch-wide felt for walls
- Two 1-yard pieces of felt in contrasting colors
- Assorted felt scraps
- Velcro® hook-and-loop tape (a 2-inch piece)
- Measuring and marking tools
- General sewing/craft supplies

The back of the house has large square windows.

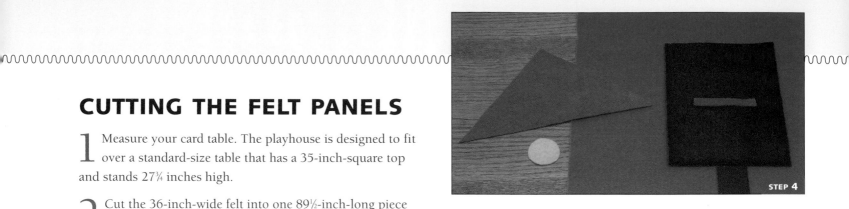

CUTTING THE FELT PANELS

1 Measure your card table. The playhouse is designed to fit over a standard-size table that has a 35-inch-square top and stands 27¾ inches high.

2 Cut the 36-inch-wide felt into one 89½-inch-long piece and two 27¾-inch-long pieces. The longer panel will drape over the tabletop and hang down two sides, to form the roof and side walls of the playhouse. The two shorter panels will become the front and back of the house. The pieces will be decorated first and then sewn together.

MAKING THE SIDE WALLS

1 For the fence, fold a sheet of copier paper in half lengthwise. Trim one end to make a rounded or pointed picket about 9¾ inches tall. Use the pattern to cut six felt pickets for each side wall, or 12 in all. Also cut two 3-inch by 36-inch strips for the fence crosspiece.

2 Sew one strip to each side wall 3½ inches above the bottom edge. Position a picket at either end, even with the bottom edge and 1 inch in from the sides. Pin in place. Pin four more pickets, evenly spaced, in between.

STEP 2

WORKROOM TIP If the felt is thin or a light color, cut two of each piece and double them up to prevent color see-through.

3 For the birdhouse, cut a 1⅜-inch by 8-inch strip for the pole, a 6-inch by 8-inch rectangle for the house, and a triangle 10 inches wide at the base and 5½ inches high for the roof. Use a large spool of thread as a template to cut a circle for the entrance hole. Cut a ½-inch by 3¼-inch strip for a perch.

STEP 4

4 Slip the pole in between the fourth and fifth pickets. Arrange the other birdhouse pieces on top, and pin in place. Topstitch all the pieces to the felt with matching thread.

WORKROOM TIP When you topstitch, line up the cut edge of the shape with the edge of your presser foot. Keep the same alignment as you stitch so that the spacing will be uniform throughout the project.

MAKING THE BACK WINDOW WALL

1 To mark the window openings, lay one of the smaller felt panels on a flat surface, the shorter edges at the sides. Measure and mark two 12-inch squares on the panel, 3½ inches apart and 10 inches from the bottom edge. (We traced around a 12-inch-square calendar.)

2 To mark the windowpanes, center a yardstick across each square, first horizontally and then vertically, and trace along both outer edges. Cut on the marked lines to make two windows with four panes each.

3 To reinforce the window openings, cut twelve 1½-inch by 15-inch strips of contrasting felt. Place two strips on each window, crisscrossing them at the center. Topstitch in place. Arrange the remaining strips around the outside edge of the windows. Overlap the strips at the corners and cut diagonally through both layers for a mitered effect. Topstitch in place. Trace around a coin to make eight contrasting felt nails. Stitch the circles to the corners of the windows.

STEP 3

4 Cut one or two free-form bushes from green felt, and stitch in place. Add any other embellishments you would like.

MAKING THE FRONT DOOR

1 Lay the remaining panel on a flat surface, shorter edges at the sides. Measuring up from the lower edge, mark two 25½-inch lines, parallel to the side edges and 18 inches apart, for the door opening. Locate the door to one side of the panel rather than in the middle (see the photo on p. 17). Cut on the two marked lines to make the door flap.

[WORKROOM TIP] Use a sliver of soap to mark lines on dark felt.

2 Cut a piece of contrasting felt the same width as and 1 inch longer than the flap. Pin it to the flap. Stitch together along the side and bottom edges. Leave the top edge pinned.

STEP 2

3 For the door tabs, cut two 7½-inch by 1½-inch strips from contrasting felt. Overlap two strips by 1 inch, and sew a 1-inch square of Velcro hook-and-loop tape to the ends. Pin two

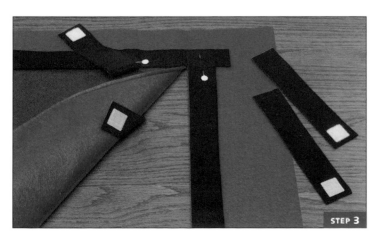
STEP 3

tabs ½ inch above the door flap and 12 inches apart. Pin their mates in the same position on the reverse side of the flap. Cut additional 1½-inch-wide strips to frame the door opening. Pin the pieces in place. Topstitch through all the layers.

4 Cut additional geometric shapes from felt to create embellishments such as a porch light, a doorbell, and a mail slot (see the photo on p. 17). Topstitch all the pieces in place. Reinforce the opening for the mail slot on both sides because it is sure to get a lot of use.

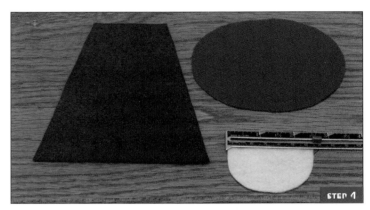
STEP 4

ASSEMBLING THE PLAYHOUSE

1 Lay the larger panel right side up on a flat surface. Measure 27¼ inches in from each short end and mark the long edge. Confirm the measurement between the marks; it should be 35 inches. Make a ⅜-inch cut into the long edge at each mark. Do this on both long edges.

2 Pin the long edges of the larger panel to the side and top edges of the two smaller panels, right sides together. Start at the bottom and work around, easing in the long piece and pivoting the corners at the clipped edges. Machine-stitch together with a ½-inch seam allowance.

STEP 2

Puppet Theater

This puppet theater can be rolled up and stored in a closet.

Young children love to put on puppet shows, and having a real puppet theater makes it even more special. The nice feature about this theater is that it can be slipped onto a spring-tension rod and set up in a doorway at a moment's notice. It is just as easily rolled up for storage when the show is over. The stage opening is positioned so that a five-year-old can kneel or sit behind the screen comfortably. Unless the theater is a surprise gift, encourage the child to help pick out the felt colors and plan how it will look.

FOR A PUPPET THEATER, YOU'LL NEED:

- 1½ yards 36-inch-wide felt or 1 yard 74-inch-wide felt
- ¼ yard each of two contrasting felt colors
- Small pieces of three additional felt colors
- Spring-tension rod to fit doorway or closet opening
- Precut sticky letters (available at Jo-Ann Fabrics) or 2-inch sign-lettering stencils (available at hardware and art supply stores)
- Measuring and marking tools
- General sewing/craft supplies

MAKING THE PANEL AND OPENING

1 For the theater panel, cut a 51-inch by 30-inch piece from the felt yardage. Fold down one short end 2 inches, and machine-stitch to form a pocket for the spring-tension rod. This will be the top of the puppet theater.

2 For the stage opening, mark a 16-inch-wide by 12-inch-high rectangle on the back of the panel, centering it 9 inches below the folded edge. Cut out the opening from the wrong side.

ADDING THE DECORATIVE ELEMENTS

1 Design a decorative edge and corners to frame the stage opening. Keep your design 2½ inches wide or less so that the edges of the opening do not become top heavy. Any design can be used. Sketch your ideas on paper first, make templates, and then cut out the pieces from felt.

2 Arrange the framing cutouts around the opening, and top-stitch in place. Reinforce the bottom corners of the opening with triangles cut from the leftover theater-panel felt.

3 Arrange purchased or hand-cut felt letters on the panel to spell out "Puppet Theater" or another message. Topstitch the letters in place.

[WORKROOM TIP] Felt is not washable, but it can be pretreated with Scotchgard® spray. To give felt pieces more body, press fusible interfacing onto the back.

Fort in a Bunk Bed

Sandra's son slept in a tent nailed to the floor of his room for a year, so sleeping in a fort sounds pretty normal to us.

FOR A BUNK BED FORT, YOU'LL NEED:

- 42- to 60-inch-wide fabric, either:

    5 yards to cover one long side and one end, or

    6¾ yards to cover one long side and two ends, or

    8¼ yards to cover two long sides and one end

- An identical amount of lining fabric
- 1-inch-wide self-adhesive Velcro hook-and-loop tape (to go around the bed frame to hang the fort panels)
- Three 1-inch-diameter Velcro hook-and-loop circles
- Two decorative buttons
- 1-inch-wide bias-tape maker
- Measuring and marking tools
- General sewing/craft supplies

Do your childhood memories include hiding out in forts? A bunk bed makes a terrific frame for a fort, creating such a cozy feeling inside that the child may never want to take the fort down. The "walls" of this fort are attached to the bed frame with Velcro hook-and-loop tape. One long side of the bed forms the front of the fort. There's an entrance flap on the right and a window flap on the left. Make plain fabric panels for the other fort walls your setup requires.

MAKING THE PANELS

1 Measure the length of the bed, jot down your figure, and call it A. Measure from the top of the lower bunk frame to the bottom of the top bunk frame; jot down this number for B. The front of the fort has two fabric panels, each the same size. The opening of the fort is between the panels. For the width of each panel, divide A by 2 and add 1 inch. For the length of each panel, add 1½ inches to B.

2 Cut two panels from your fort fabric and two panels from your lining fabric to the measurements calculated in step 1. If you are making other solid panels, calculate their dimensions now and cut out the pieces.

[**WORKROOM TIP**] Keep a tablet of graph paper near your sewing machine. Jot down your measurements and notes for every project you make, even if you are just experimenting. At a later date when you want to do a similar project, these notes will save you time.

3 Place the fort and lining panels right sides together in pairs. Machine-stitch around three sides with a ½-inch seam allowance, leaving the top edge open. Clip off the corners of the seam allowance. Turn right side out. Press well. Stitch the top raw edges together.

MAKING THE WINDOW AND DOOR FLAP

1 For the window, mark a 12-inch square in the middle of one front panel. Cut out the opening. Finish the raw edges of the window opening with 1-inch-wide self-bias tape.

STEP 1

2 For the window flap, cut one 14½-inch by 16-inch piece from the fort fabric and one from the lining. Stitch right sides together, leaving the top edge open. Clip the corners, turn right side out, and press. Serge the top raw edges. Press the serged edge 1 inch toward the lining. Set the window flap aside.

STEP 2

3 For the window tabs, cut two 10-inch by 2½-inch strips from the fort fabric and two from the lining. Place the strips right sides together in pairs. Machine-stitch around three sides with a ½-inch seam allowance, forming a point at one end. Trim the seam allowance, turn right side out, and press. Tuck in the raw edges and hand-sew closed. On the pointed end, sew a Velcro circle to the lining side and a button to the right side. Sew the Velcro hook-and-loop mate to the other end of the strip on the right side. The two ends should come together in a circle.

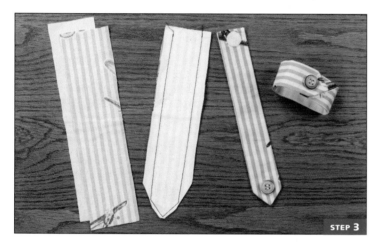

4 To complete the window, lay the large panel flat, right side up. Center the window flap over the opening, the folded edge at the top. Turn the two flaps facedown, and slip them under the flap, one at each side, so the pointed ends extend 3 inches beyond the window opening at the top. Pin all the pieces in place. Topstitch the flap ¼ inch from the folded edge through all layers. Underneath, the tabs will be caught in the topstitching.

5 Lift the flap. Fold in and press the serged edge. Pin to hold the fold, and topstitch.

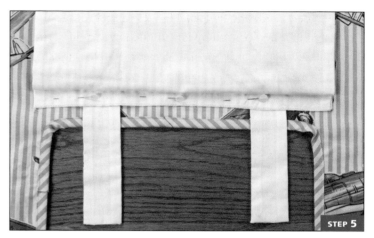

6 Roll the flap under toward the lining side. Secure the window tabs around the rolled flap with the hook-and-loop circles.

COMPLETING THE FORT

1 For the fort door flap, use the other front panel made in step 3 on p. 23. Lay the panel facedown and sew a short piece of Velcro hook-and-loop tape to the lower right corner. The right edge is the fort opening. Make a 4-inch-long tab from scrap fabric, sew the Velcro mate to one end, and sew the tab to the top edge of the panel 27 inches in from the right edge.

STEP 1

2 To set up the fort, use a glue gun to attach a long strip of Velcro to the top bunk, along the lower inside edge of the frame. Glue or sew matching strips to the window and door panels. Repeat for any other plain panels that you made. Hang the panels as shown in the photo on p. 22. To hold the door open, bring the lower corner up to the tab and let the Velcro hook-and-loop pieces connect.

Hang the panels as shown in the photo on p. 22.

TRICK of the TRADE

MAKING BIAS TAPE

Strips of fabric with the long edges folded in can be used as a decorative band on window treatments, to edge the skirts of ottomans or slipcovers, or as ties to hold a cushion in place. You can purchase bias tape in solid colors for this purpose, but for more color and fabric variety, it's practical to make your own. Tape made from striped fabric, for example, produces an interesting diagonal stripe effect.

You'll need a bias-tape maker, a small metal tool sold at notions counters for about $5. It comes in different sizes to make a finished single-fold bias tape ½ inch to 2 inches wide. A single-fold tape has both long edges folded in. A double-fold tape is made by folding a single-fold tape almost in half, so the edges are offset slightly.

Cut your bias strips the required width for your tool, and seam them together end to end on the straight grain so the seams run diagonally across the strip. Cut one end of the strip on an angle. Use a pin to pass this pointed end through the broad end of the bias-tape maker and out the tapered end. Watch the bias-tape maker do its magic. Work at the ironing board so you can press the folds into place as you go.

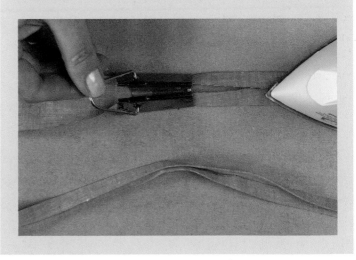

Birdcage Cover and Seed Catcher

Birds, while fun, can be noisy and messy. Sometimes you might like to enjoy a quiet visit with a friend without the bird's accompaniment. Covering the cage with a towel is not the most attractive option. And it's not much fun to vacuum up birdseed under the cage several times a day. Why not make a birdcage cover and seed catcher to solve both these problems at once?

FOR A BIRDCAGE COVER, YOU'LL NEED:

- Birdcage with an arched top (Tenwood® Cage #1209 APC shown)
- ¾ yard fabric
- ¾ yard lining fabric
- ¾ yard muslin or scrap fabric
- 1¼ yards fringe
- 2¼ yards decorative cord

FOR THE SEED CATCHER, YOU'LL NEED:

- ½ yard fabric
- ½ yard lining fabric
- 2 yards elastic

FOR BOTH:

- Measuring and marking tools
- General sewing/craft supplies

Making a birdcage cover with a curved top is easy. Once you know the technique, you'll be able to tackle anything from a blender to a pinball machine.

A fabric seed catcher hugs the cage, thanks to elastic in the casings.

MAKING THE BIRDCAGE COVER

1 Set the back of the birdcage on brown paper or newspaper. Trace around the curved edge, down to the widest point where the wire joins the plastic base. Trace a line even with the bottom of the cage, extending it to each side. Set the cage aside.

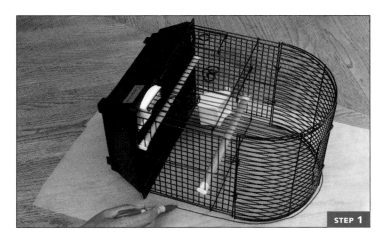

2 Use a ruler to straighten the traced lines and extend each curved line straight down to meet the bottom line. Add a ½-inch seam allowance all around. Cut out the pattern; fold and retrim as needed to make the pattern symmetrical. Label the pattern Front/Back.

3 For the second pattern piece, draw a rectangle. To determine the width, measure across the cage side wall from front to back and add 1 inch, or two ½-inch seam allowances on each long edge. For the length, measure the entire curved section as shown and add 1 inch. Label this pattern Top/Sides.

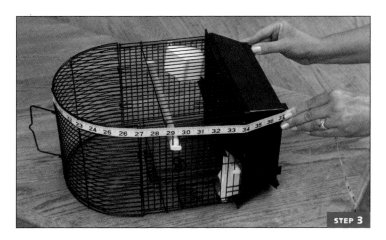

4 To test-fit the patterns, cut one back, one front, and one top/sides piece from muslin or scrap fabric. Notch the top center of the front and back and the middle of the long edges on the rectangle. Machine-baste the pieces together, matching the notches and making ½-inch seams.

5 Try the cover on the cage inside out. It should be fairly loose so that it can slip on and off easily but not so big that the bird can pull pieces of cloth inside the cage. Make any needed adjustments.

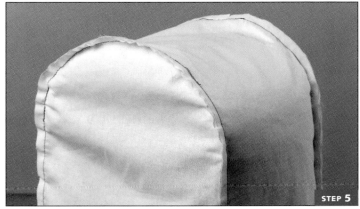

6 Take out the basting stitches. Use the muslin pieces as patterns to cut one cage back, one cage front, and one rectangle from the cage fabric. Cut a matching set of pieces from the lining fabric.

7 Sew the decorative cord around the curved edge of the cage front and back, using a Pearls 'N Piping™ or a zipper foot. Clip into the lip around the curves so the cord lies flat.

8 Pin the front and back to the rectangle, right sides together, matching the center notches and ends. Ease in the fullness in between, and place on the machine bed with the larger piece against the feed dogs. Use a zipper foot to stitch in close to the decorative cord. Sew the three lining pieces together in the same way.

9 Place the lining and cover right sides together, matching the seams and bottom edges. Machine-stitch 1 inch from the bottom edge all around, leaving a 5-inch opening for turning. Turn right side out through the opening, push the lining down inside the cover, and sew the opening closed. Test-fit the cover on the birdcage. Pin the fringe to the lower edge, and topstitch in place.

10 To make an opening for the cage handle, put the cover on the cage, feel for where the handle starts and stops, and mark with chalk. Make a very large buttonhole at this spot, or cut the opening and zigzag the edges. Top with decorative fringe.

STEP 10

MAKING THE SEED CATCHER

1 Measure around the bottom of the birdcage, and multiply by 2½. Cut a strip this length by 6 inches wide from both the seed catcher and lining fabrics, piecing as needed to obtain the required length.

2 Place the strips right sides together and sew the long edges, to make a tube. Insert a yardstick or pressing stick inside the tube and press the seams open.

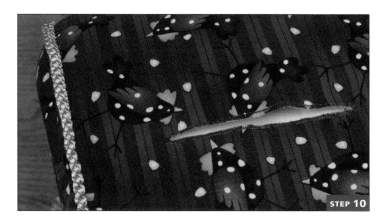

STEP 2

3 Trim the seam allowances to ⅛ inch along the edges of the strips to ease the passage of the elastic. Turn the tube right side out and press flat. Fold in the edges ⅜ inch at one end and press flat. To make the casings, machine-stitch ⅜ inch in from the edge down both long sides, stopping 1 inch from the folded end.

STEP 3

4 Cut a piece of elastic to fit around the bottom of the cage; the fit should be loose, not tight or stretched. Use a bodkin or safety pin to draw the elastic through the casing, entering at the raw edge. When the fabric starts scrunching up, tack the free end of the elastic even with the raw edge of the casing to prevent it from pulling through. Continue the insertion, taking care that the elastic does not roll, until the safety pin emerges out the folded end. Remove the safety pin, overlap the two elastic ends to form a ring, and stitch together. Don't allow the folded end of the casing to get caught in the stitching. Repeat for the casing on the opposite side.

STEP 4

5 Double-check to make sure the elastic joins are secure, and restitch if needed. Pull the folded edge over the joins to conceal them, and hand-sew so the folded edge lies flat. Stretch the seed catcher slightly to put it on the birdcage. Slide it down to the base so that it can catch any seed the bird kicks around.

Cozy Dog Bed

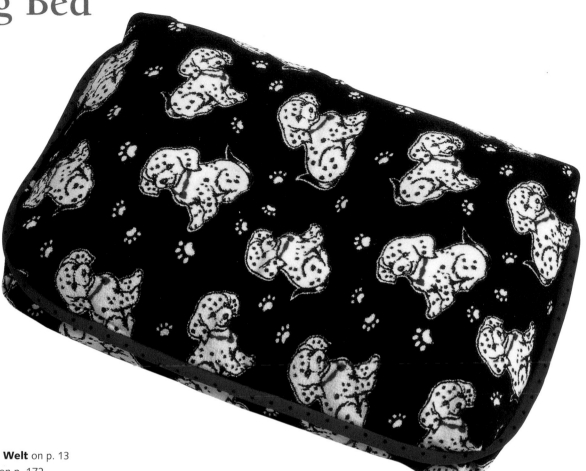

The cushion inside this dog bed is an ordinary bed pillow.

Before You Begin see **Single Welt** on p. 13 and **Sewing Zippers into Seams** on p. 172.

FOR ONE DOG BED, YOU'LL NEED:

- Standard, queen, or king bed pillow (depending on the size of dog)
- ¾ yard to 1 yard of fabric for cover
- Fabric and ⅜-inch cord for welt
- Upholstery thread or dental floss
- Fabric glue
- 20-inch zipper and ¼-inch double-sided zipper adhesive tape (optional)
- Long doll-making needle
- Measuring and marking tools
- General sewing/craft supplies

Commercial dog beds will always be available, but ours is softer and cozier and matches the room decor. The filler is an ordinary bed pillow. Choose a pillow size—standard, queen, or king—that is appropriate for your dog. Most bed pillows are washable, and with a zipper insertion in the seam, it will be easy to keep the cushion clean and fresh. The cover can be sewn from cotton flannel, polyfleece, or even washable faux fur. Flannel fabric should be preshrunk in hot water before you begin the construction; if you don't, the cushion cover will shrink and draw up the welt cord with the first washing. It is not necessary to preshrink polyfleece, faux fur, or welt cord.

PREPARING THE PILLOW

1 Plump up the pillow. Using a tape measure, measure the pillow length and width, from seam to seam, without crushing the loft. Jot down your figures. Add 2½ inches to each measurement to allow for ease, seam allowances, and a zipper application. Cut two pieces of fabric to these dimensions for the dog bed cover. By giving the cover a loose fit, the dog will be able to sink into the pillow and be really cozy.

[WORKROOM TIP] Serge the outside edge of each cushion cover piece before you begin construction to give the seams a clean finish. This way, the cover will stand up to frequent washings without fraying. Always close the zipper before laundering the cover.

2 Shape the pillow into a cushion. First, shake out any filler lodged in the corners. Flatten each corner by bringing the seams together. Fold the corner perpendicular to the seamline about 3 inches from the corner point. Press this triangular flap against the pillow, and hand-sew or glue in place with fabric glue, securing with straight pins until the glue dries.

3 Thread a long doll-making needle with upholstery thread or dental floss. Make four or five stitches 3 inches apart in the center of the pillow. Go through all the layers, drawing the thread just enough to create a hollowed indent in the middle of the pillow.

MAKING THE COVER AND WELT

1 Make Turkish corners on the two cover pieces cut in step 1 above. Fold each corner back on itself, right side in and raw edges matching. Measure 3 inches in from the corner point, and stitch perpendicular to the cut edge for ⅜ inch.

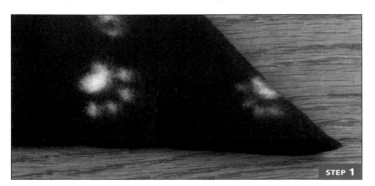
STEP 1

2 To complete each corner, open out and flatten the fullness. Stitch across the lower edge.

STEP 2

3 Use the ⅜-inch-diameter welt cord and contrasting fabric to make 3¼ yards of covered welt or enough to go around the cushion. The lip should be 1 inch wide if you plan to install a zipper, ⅜ inch wide if not.

4 Sew the welt around the top cover, right sides together and edges matching, butting and joining the ends when you reach the starting point. Clip into the lip as needed to enable the welt to turn the corners.

STEP 4

COMPLETING THE DOG BED

1 Insert a zipper between the top and bottom covers at this point, if desired. Continue stitching all around to complete the cushion cover. If no zipper is desired, stitch the covers right sides together along the welt stitching line, leaving a 20-inch opening.

2 Turn the cover right side out, insert the pillow, and distribute the fullness. Zip closed or sew the opening by hand.

Litter Box Cover

Not everyone has a discreet place to hide a kitty litter box, so it often ends up in plain view. By making the box more attractive, it can actually become a feature in your overall decor. A litter box cover also makes an offbeat housewarming gift for a cat owner. Buy a new litter box and make the cover to go with it.

Before You Begin see **Single Welt** on p. 13 and **Making Bias Tape** on p. 25.

FOR ONE LITTER BOX COVER, YOU'LL NEED:

- Litter box cover and pan
- 1⅝ yards fabric
- 1⅝ yards lining fabric
- 1⅝ yards muslin or scrap fabric
- Fringe to go around box opening
- Fabric and ¼-inch cord for welt and binding
- 2½ yards fleece
- Marking and measuring tools
- General sewing/craft supplies

A bright red print and a decorative diagonal seam give an ordinary kitty litter box an oriental theme.

MAKING THE PATTERNS

1 Remove the litter box cover from the pan. Turn the cover upside down on brown paper or newspaper and trace around the top. In the same way, turn the cover on its side to trace the side wall and the front wall, including the opening where the cat enters. These two pieces will probably be broad at the bottom and taper slightly at the top. Label the three patterns Top, Side, and Front/Back. Indicate which are the top and bottom edges, where appropriate.

2 Extend the bottom edges of the Side and Front/Back pattern outlines, to account for the extra depth of the litter box pan. Use a ruler to straighten the traced lines and verify that the corners will line up when the pieces are sewn together. Add ½ inch all around for a seam allowance, except on the bottom edges. Cut out all three patterns. Fold and retrim as needed to make the patterns symmetrical.

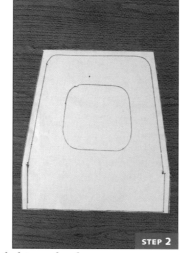

STEP 2

3 To test-fit the patterns, cut one top, two sides, one back, and one front from muslin. Machine-baste the sides to the top, and then join the front and back, making ½-inch seams.

4 Try the cover on the litter box inside out, checking the length and the ease in moving the cover on and off the box. Make any needed adjustments. Take out the basting stitches so that you can use the muslin pieces as patterns.

CUTTING AND SEWING THE COVER

1 Draw a diagonal line across the top right corner of the front pattern, for a decorative shoulder seam. Cut the pattern apart. Add a ½-inch seam allowance to each cut edge by pinning or taping paper to it.

2 Using all the patterns, cut one front, one front corner, one top, one back, and two sides from the decorative fabric. Tape the front pattern pieces back together, and cut one top, one back, one front, and two sides from the lining fabric and the fleece. Do not cut out the front opening on the lining and fleece pieces yet.

3 Use the welt cord and contrasting fabric to make 6 yards of covered welt. The lip should be ½ inch wide.

4 Using a zipper foot, stitch a short piece of welt to the angled edge of the front corner. Sew the front and front corner together, right sides facing, enclosing the welt in the seam.

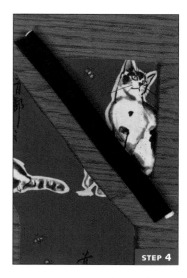

STEP 4

5 Back each decorative fabric piece with its fleece mate. Hand-baste or glue in place.

6 Use needle-nose pliers to pull out ½ inch of cord at each end of the angled seam. Clip off this bit of cord with scissors to reduce bulk. Let the remainder disappear back inside the welt covering. Sew welt around the side and top edges of the front, leaving the straight bottom edge plain. Clip into the lip as needed to enable the welt to turn the corners. Trim the back piece with welt in the same way. Also sew welt to the top piece where it will join the sides.

STEP 6

STEP 7

STEP 8

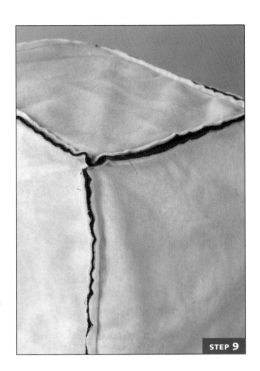

STEP 9

7 Pin the fringe around the opening of the front piece. Machine-stitch all around along the lip of the fringe. If the fringe looks skimpy, add a second round.

8 Pin the front lining to the front piece, right sides together. With the fleece facing up, machine-stitch around the opening over the previous stitching. Trim the seam allowance to ¼ inch. Clip the curves. Turn the lining to the wrong side so that the fringe falls into the opening. Press.

9 Join the two side pieces to the top, using a zipper foot to sew close to the welt. Then add the front and back. Keep the front lining clear of these seams.

10 Sew the lining top, sides, and back together. Sew the remaining side and top edges to the lining front, which is already attached to the cover. Turn the cover right side out, with the lining snuggled inside.

11 Slip the cover over the litter box and check the length. The raw edge should be even and clear the floor by ½ inch. Machine-stitch ¼ inch from the edge to join the layers together. Make bias tape from the remaining welt fabric, and bind the edge.

STEP 11

Part 2 SEATING

Is there ever enough seating in our homes for the few occasions when we need to accommodate a crowd? Hassocks, floor pillows, and floor cushions can provide just the extra seating you are looking for, and they are easy to make. They also make welcome housewarming gifts for your son or daughter's first apartment. Maybe your kitchen chairs or bar stools are due for a makeover, or you would like to encourage guests to linger after dinner with some really comfy boxed cushions for your dining room chairs. If you can sit on it, you can cover it.

Faux-Leather Hassock

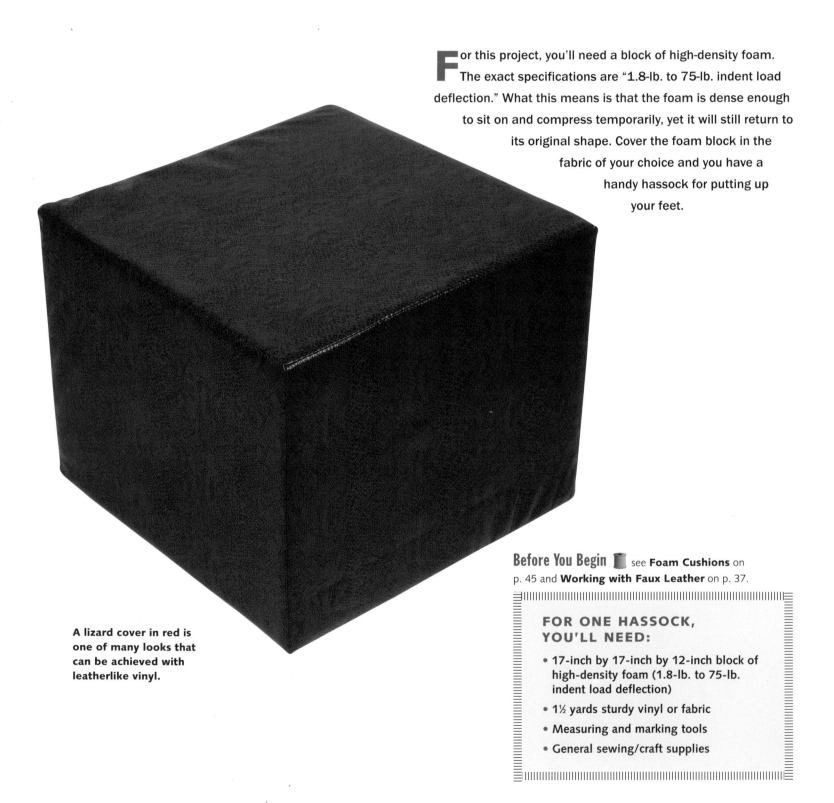

For this project, you'll need a block of high-density foam. The exact specifications are "1.8-lb. to 75-lb. indent load deflection." What this means is that the foam is dense enough to sit on and compress temporarily, yet it will still return to its original shape. Cover the foam block in the fabric of your choice and you have a handy hassock for putting up your feet.

A lizard cover in red is one of many looks that can be achieved with leatherlike vinyl.

Before You Begin see **Foam Cushions** on p. 45 and **Working with Faux Leather** on p. 37.

FOR ONE HASSOCK, YOU'LL NEED:

- 17-inch by 17-inch by 12-inch block of high-density foam (1.8-lb. to 75-lb. indent load deflection)
- 1½ yards sturdy vinyl or fabric
- Measuring and marking tools
- General sewing/craft supplies

CUTTING THE PIECES

1 Measure the top and bottom of the block to verify that each square measures 17 inches by 17 inches. Cut two 18-inch by 18-inch squares of fabric, or ½ inch larger than the block top all around, for the top and bottom panels. For a block of different dimensions, adjust the cut fabric size accordingly.

2 Measure the block sides to verify that each one is 12 inches by 17 inches. Cut four 13-inch by 18-inch pieces of fabric, or ½ inch larger than one side all around, for the side panels. As in step 1, adjust the size as needed.

COMPLETING THE HASSOCK

1 Place two side panels right sides together, edges matching. Sew along a 13-inch edge with a ½-inch seam allowance, stopping and back-tacking ½ inch from the edge at each end. Repeat to join all four side panels in a continuous loop.

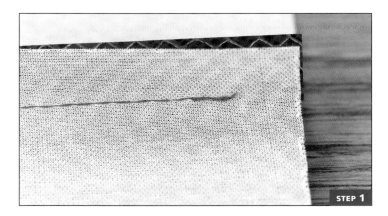

STEP 1

2 Press the seams open; vinyl should be finger-pressed rather than ironed because an iron will melt vinyl. Pin the top panel to the side pieces, right sides together. The loose ½-inch seam allowance at the ends will allow you to pivot around the corners. Stitch together with a ½-inch seam allowance.

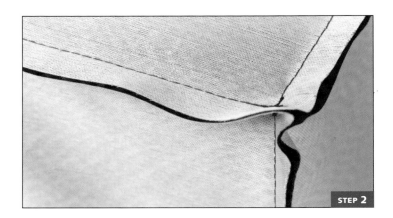

STEP 2

3 Test-fit the cover on the foam block, wrapping the block with a plastic dry cleaner's bag for easy insertion. The fit should be snug. Remove the foam block.

4 Press (or finger-press) three edges of the bottom panel ½ inch to the wrong side. Sew the fourth edge to the cover, leaving the three pressed edges unattached for the foam insertion. Trim all the seams close to the stitching to reduce bulk. Trim out the corners. Turn the cover right side out.

5 Insert the foam block in the cover, using plastic so it glides in easily. Reach inside and smooth out the seam allowances so that they lie on one side or the other. Be sure to remove all the plastic. Tuck the raw edges under the folded edges of the bottom panel, and pin together. Hand-sew closed, spacing the stitches ¼ inch apart.

SCRAPS of Knowledge

WORKING WITH FAUX LEATHER

Always sew and press a sample of your faux leather before you actually begin the project. Use a long stitch length to avoid closely spaced needle holes that will weaken the seam. If sticking is a problem, switch to a Teflon or roller presser foot. Pressing with an iron is not recommended; finger-press instead. To hand-sew faux leather, tape the pieces together instead of pinning them. Use a glover needle, which has a wedge-shaped point, to pierce through the dense material. You might be tempted to use upholstery thread, but don't—it requires a bigger needle, which will leave bigger holes.

Floor Pillows

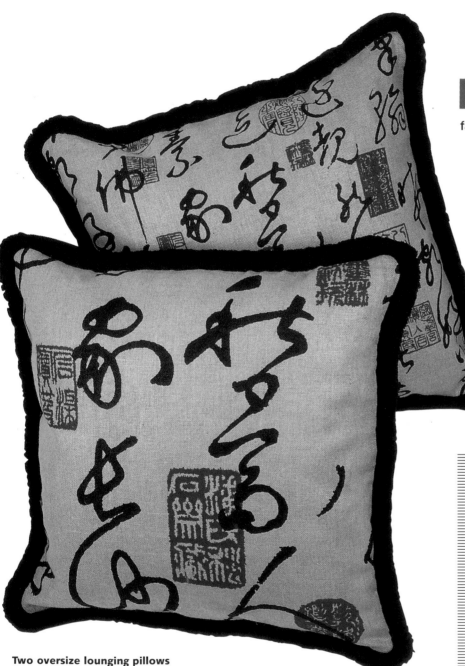

Floor pillows are sought after for casual sitting and especially for TV watching. They're fast and easy to make—just think of them as giant throw pillows. The large size demands a hefty edging. A 2-inch-wide fringe, doubled and enclosed in the seam, does the job. Another option is a hefty 1-inch-diameter welt cord covered with a contrasting fabric. No attempt is made to install a zipper in seams this bulky. Instead, the open edge is sewn closed by hand.

Two oversize lounging pillows each measure 30 inches square. For even bigger pillows, use 36-inch-square pillow forms.

FOR EACH PILLOW, YOU'LL NEED:

- 30-inch-square pillow form
- 2 yards fabric, or 1 yard each of two different fabrics
- 7 yards fringe (to be sewn as a double layer)
- Measuring and marking tools
- General sewing/craft supplies

PREPARING THE PILLOWS

1 Measure the pillow from seam to seam in both directions. Jot down your figures. Cut a pillow front and back to these exact dimensions for a finished pillow that is extra firm. For a softer pillow, add ½ inch to the pillow dimensions all around.

2 Tape the ends of the fringe to keep it intact. Tape the middle of the fringe. Cut through the tape, making two equal lengths. Hold both fringe lips together and treat them as one unit.

MAKING THE PILLOWS

1 Lay the pillow front right side up on the sewing machine bed. Place the lip of the fringe on the fabric edge with the fringe facing in toward the middle of the pillow; it is not necessary to pin. Set the machine for a long stitch length. Going slowly, stitch the fringe to the pillow front, just beyond the inside row of stitching on the lip. When you reach a corner, snip the outer row of stitching on the lip as needed to ease the fringe around the corner.

STEP 1

2 Continue sewing the fringe to the pillow front all around until you are near the starting point. To end off, you will be butting the fringe ends, not overlaying them. Determine where the butt will occur, tape the fringe lip, and make clean cuts. Remove the tape just before you sew the lip to the fabric to keep the fringe intact.

3 Press one long edge of the pillow back ½ inch to the wrong side, for the pillow opening. Place the back and front right sides together. Pin in place, with the pillow front on top, making sure the fringe is turned toward the inside.

4 Machine-stitch ½ inch from the edge all around, starting and stopping 1½ inches past the corners on the side that has the folded edge, to create a 27-inch opening. If you find the bottom fabric layer is sliding out, remove the work from the machine, hand-baste all around, and then resume the machine sewing.

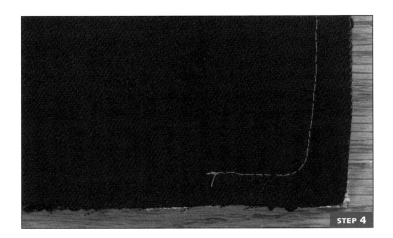
STEP 4

5 Trim the corners diagonally to eliminate bulk. Turn the pillow cover right side out. Insert the pillow form. Thread a hand needle with a double thread. Hand-sew the opening closed, making the stitches ¼ inch apart.

DESIGN IDEA Before you hand-sew, run the thread across a small cake of beeswax, available at notions counters. Press the thread with a warm iron to set the beeswax. The wax coating will make the thread stronger and help it glide through the fabric.

SCRAPS of Knowledge

AVOIDING NEEDLE BREAKAGE

When multiple layers of fabric and trim become so thick that you can hardly slide them under the presser foot, breaking a needle is a strong possibility. Needle breakage occurs when you try to push or pull the fabric to move the sewing along. The needle gets pulled out of alignment and hits the plate instead of passing down through the throat hole to make its connection with the bobbin. To prevent the needle from wandering off course, let the feed dogs move the fabric along slowly. Make adjustments only when the needle is in the up position, out of the fabric.

Floor Cushions

Floor cushions are similar to floor pillows except that the corners are boxed. If you need extra floor seating, it is interesting to combine the two styles. These cushions were sewn from vinyl.

Make a pair of vinyl cushions, swapping their colors for the contrasting welt.

Before You Begin see **Foam Cushions** on p. 45, **Sewing with Vinyl** on p. 189, **Single Welt** on p. 13, and **Sewing Zippers into Seams** on p. 172.

FOR EACH FLOOR CUSHION, YOU'LL NEED:

- 4-inch-thick foam, cut to a 22-inch square
- 2 yards bonded batting
- 1¾ yards vinyl
- Thin vinyl and ½-inch cord for welt
- 27-inch zipper
- Spray adhesive
- Measuring and marking tools
- General sewing/craft supplies

PREPARING THE PIECES

1 Wrap the batting around the 22-inch square of foam in a single layer. Cut the edges so that they can be butted together. Cut out the excess batting for a smooth fit at the corners. Affix the batting to the foam using spray adhesive. If the adhesive doesn't hold, whip the edges together by hand. Your goal is to make a sealed, smooth cushion cover.

2 Measure once around the entire cushion. Divide the measurement by 2 and add 1 inch. Cut two vinyl squares to this dimension for the cushion top and bottom.

[**WORKROOM TIP**] Exact measuring is important with vinyl—don't count on any ease with this fabric. To sew vinyl, set your machine stitch to almost a basting length. Too many stitches in vinyl will weaken the seams.

SEWING THE CUSHION

1 Fold each corner back on itself, right side in and raw edges matching. Measure 2 inches in from the corner point, and stitch perpendicular to the cut edge for 1 inch.

2 To complete each corner, open out and flatten the fullness. Stitch across the lower edge, and trim off the excess.

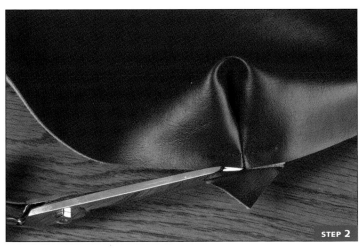

3 Use the welt cord and thin vinyl to make enough welt to go around the edge of the cushion. Join the welt to the top cushion, butting the ends.

STEP 4a

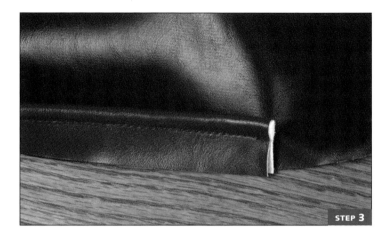

STEP 3

[WORKROOM TIP] The first time you make a welted cushion or pillow, use the smaller ¼-inch-diameter cord. It's easier to work with.

STEP 4b

4 Sew a zipper to the welted edge to go along one side of the cushion and around the two corners for 3 inches. Leave 1 inch at each end of the zipper unstitched. Join the cushion front and back together for 3 inches at each end, and complete the zipper installation.

5 Unzip the zipper about halfway. Pin the cushion front and back right sides together, matching up the corners. Machine-stitch all around close to the welting. Turn right side out. Open the zipper completely, and insert the cushion. Zip closed.

STEP 4c

Bar Stool Cushion

Making covers for kitchen stool seats can give a breakfast bar or counter area a brand new look. Choose a vinyl or vinylized fabric so the stools can be wiped clean with a damp sponge. There are many exciting fabric designs available.

Before You Begin see **Foam Cushions** on p. 45, **Single Welt** on p. 13, and **What Is Boxing?** on p. 50.

FOR EACH STOOL CUSHION, YOU'LL NEED:

- Bar stool with a flat seat
- 2-inch-thick foam, cut to match seat
- ½-inch-thick plywood, cut to match seat
- ⅝ yard vinyl or vinylized fabric
- Fabric and ¼-inch cord for welt
- 1 package Industrial Strength Sticky Back® Velcro
- Staple gun with ½-inch staples
- Measuring and marking tools
- General sewing/craft supplies

Stools are more comfortable with thick padded cushions.

SEWING THE
CUSHION COVER

1 Turn your stool upside down on a sheet of newspaper. Trace around the edge of the seat. Cut out the shape on the marked line to make a pattern. Use the pattern to cut a matching shape from 2-inch-thick foam and ½-inch-thick plywood. Ask the foam shop and lumberyard to cut these pieces for you.

2 Place the pattern on the vinyl fabric, and cut ½ inch beyond the edge all around for the seat cover. Measure around the edge of the pattern with a tape measure, and add 6 inches. Cut a boxing strip to this length by 4½ inches wide.

3 Use the fabric and ¼-inch cord to make enough welt to go around the seat cover. Sew the welt in place, butting and joining the ends. Clip into the lip to ease the welt around the curved edge as needed.

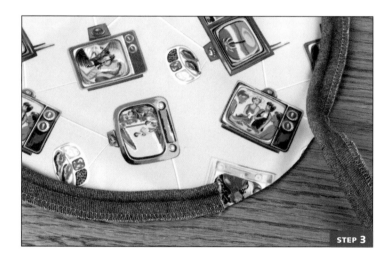

STEP 3

4 Place the seat cover and boxing strip together, right sides facing and edges matching, with the seat cover on top. Using a zipper foot, begin sewing 3 inches from the end of the boxing strip along the welt stitching, to join the pieces together. You won't need pins if you sew slowly and glide the boxing strip along the curved seat edge.

STEP 4

5 Sew all around, stopping when you are 3 inches from your starting point. Back-tack and remove the work from the machine. Hand-walk the ends of the boxing strip toward each other along the remaining edge, and mark where they meet. Seam the ends together. Trim the seam allowance to ¼ inch. Return to the machine, and finish sewing the last few inches of the boxing strip to the seat. Trim the seam allowance to ¼ inch. Turn the seat cover right side out.

ASSEMBLING THE CUSHION

1 Turn the seat cover upside down. Insert the 2-inch foam shape inside, and flatten the seam allowance toward the boxing strip. Next, slip in the plywood.

STEP **1**

2 Smooth the excess fabric onto the plywood. Staple about 1 inch in from the plywood edge, first on one side and then on the other side. Repeat so that there are four staples evenly spaced around the edge. Staple the areas in between in the same way. Cut off the excess fabric close to the staples so that the seat will lie flat on top of the stool.

3 Affix the Sticky Back Velcro hook-and-loop fastener to the exposed plywood. Affix the Velcro mate to the stool seat to hold the cushion in place.

STEP **3**

Kitchen Chair Seat Covers

Cover six chair seats in two hours by trading in your sewing machine for a staple gun.

If you have noticed that your kitchen or dining room chairs are looking a bit shabby, why not re-cover them? To get a good color match for the room, snip off some rug pile to take with you to the fabric store. When you have a color base to start with, a coordinating fabric is a lot easier to spot. If the room is sunny, avoid dark colors as these tend to fade quickly.

Before You Begin see **Foam Cushions** on page 45.

FOR EACH PADDED SEAT COVER, YOU'LL NEED:

- Fabric
- 1-inch-thick batting
- ½-inch-thick foam
- Staple gun with ⅜-inch staples
- Hammer
- Screwdriver
- Spray adhesive
- Measuring and marking tools

PREPARING THE SEAT

1 Turn the chair over, and unscrew and remove the seat. Remove any existing cover and padding material from the seat and discard them.

2 Trace around the seat to make a paper pattern. Mark a line 3 inches beyond the seat outline all around. Cut on the outside line to make the seat pattern. Use the pattern to determine how much foam, batting, and fabric you will need.

STEP 2

[**WORKROOM TIP**] If your chair frame is missing the seat, cut a replacement from ½-inch-thick plywood. You can also make a plywood seat for chairs that don't have a removable seat. Cut the plywood ½ inch smaller than the existing seat all around to allow for the bulk of the foam, batting, and fabric.

3 Use the seat as a template to cut a matching piece of ½-inch-thick foam. For extra padding, cut one or more pieces of 1-inch-thick batting 1½ inches larger than the seat all around. An exception is if the seat is one that sinks down into the chair frame. In this case, cut the batting even with the seat edge, to fit the opening.

MAKING THE SEAT COVER

1 Use spray adhesive to affix the foam to the top of the seat. Lay the batting on a flat work surface, and apply a light coat of spray adhesive. Center the seat foam side down on the batting, and press gently to adhere.

2 Use the paper pattern to cut one seat cover from fabric. Lay the fabric piece facedown. Center the padded seat facedown on top of it.

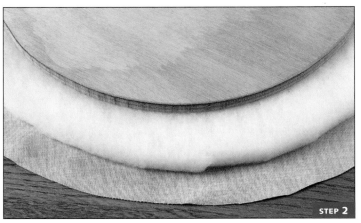

STEP 2

[**WORKROOM TIP**] If you are covering several chairs with a patterned or napped fabric, make a notation on the paper pattern and position it on the fabric the same way each time, so that all the covers will look alike.

3 Working on grain, draw two opposite edges of the fabric and batting up onto the underside of the seat, and staple in place about 1½ inches from the edge. Repeat on the crossgrain, stapling down two more edges on opposite sides of the seat. Continue in this way, stapling first one side and then the other, pulling the fabric taut as you go. Space the staples about 1 inch apart. If the seat is square, start at the middle of each edge and work out to the corners. Corners can be finished by folding one edge over the other, pulling the fabric smooth, and stapling down.

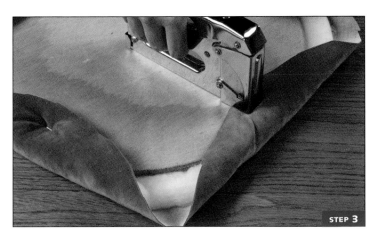

STEP 3

4 Cut off any excess fabric beyond the staples. Reposition the newly covered seat on the chair and screw in place from the underside.

Boxed Cushions for Dining Chairs

With its added height and well-defined shape, a box cushion looks more elegant than a plain chair pad. The skirt can be either pleated or gathered. Omit the skirt altogether to focus attention on the handsome welted seams. If you go a step further and pick contrasting fabrics for the cushion top and bottom, you'll get a new look simply by flipping the cushion over. By choosing your own design details and cutting your own pattern, you'll be able to have custommade cushions that perfectly suit the character and shape of your chairs.

Before You Begin see **Foam Cushions** on p. 45, **Single Welt** on p. 13, and **What Is Boxing?** on p. 50.

FOR ONE CHAIR PAD, YOU'LL NEED:

- 1 yard fabric, plus extra for skirt
- Fabric and ¼-inch cord for welt
- 1½- to 2-inch-thick foam
- 1-inch-thick batting
- Foam & Fabric Adhesive #581 (available at foam shops)
- General sewing/craft supplies

Boxed cushions will encourage your family and friends to linger at the dining room table because they make the chairs so comfy.

SIZING THE CUSHION

1 Cover the chair seat with a large sheet of paper (newspaper is always handy for this purpose), and trace the seat edge all around. If the seat has a raised edge or lip to hold a cushion in place, reduce the pattern by ¼ inch in order to accommodate the welt. Even a narrow welt takes up space, and if it is not accounted for, the fit will be too snug.

2 Cut out the seat pattern. Fold it in half and trim both edges at once so that each side is the mirror image of the other. Open the pattern, place it on the chair seat, and double-check the pattern size and shape. By making the pattern symmetrical, you'll be able to flip the cushion over when one side gets soiled, when you want a style or color change, or to promote even wear.

WHAT IS BOXING?

Boxing is a strip of fabric that makes a shape three-dimensional. When the top and bottom of a cushion cover are joined to a boxing strip, instead of directly to each other, the shape becomes fuller and more defined. A matching or contrasting welt enhances the definition even further and makes for a professional finish. The boxing strip fabric does not have to match the cushion top and bottom; a contrasting boxing adds interest and also sidesteps the difficulty of trying to continue a pattern across a seamline. The width of the cut boxing strip is the depth of the cushion plus 1 inch for seam allowances. The length is the circumference around the cushion plus 1 inch.

3 Use the pattern to cut a matching shape from 1½- to 2-inch-thick foam. Cut a piece of 1-inch-thick batting to match, and fuse it to the top of the cushion using Foam & Fabric Adhesive #581.

DESIGNING AND SEWING THE COVER

1 Use the seat pattern to cut out a top and a bottom piece for the cushion cover, adding a ½-inch seam allowance all around. Use matching or contrasting fabrics.

2 Cut a matching or contrasting boxing strip to fit around the cushion plus 1 inch. Make the strip 1 inch wider than the cushion depth, for a ½-inch seam allowance at the top and bottom edges. For the ties, cut two 34-inch-long pieces two times the boxing strip width plus 1 inch.

3 Use the welt cord and bias-cut strips of fabric to make enough welt to go around both cushion cover pieces plus 10 inches extra. Machine-baste the welt around the edge of the cushion top and bottom, starting and ending at the back edge. Be sure to stitch the corners identically. Join the welt ends together to eliminate bulk. For a cushion cover without a skirt, go to step 9.

4 To design a chair skirt, experiment with scrap fabric on the chair. Just as skirt styles differ on women, a skirt may or may not flatter a particular chair. Pleated corners are tailored and work well with crisp or heavy fabrics. A gathered skirt is suitable for lightweight fabrics. Typically, a skirt is either 5 inches long or goes to the floor. A skirt may run on three sides only or include an extra panel at the back, depending on the chair construction. Once you've decided on a style, a length, and how many sides to cover, go on to step 5.

5 Measure around the edges of the foam cushion where the skirt will be applied. For pleated corners, add 24 inches or enough for two pleats taking up 12 inches total at each front corner. For a gathered skirt, multiply the edge measurement by 2½. For the length, double the skirt height and add 1 inch for the seam allowances. Cut the skirt fabric to these dimensions, piecing as necessary to obtain the required fullness. With a bit of calculating, you can position the seams to fall at the pleat folds.

6 Fold the skirt fabric in half lengthwise, right side in. At each end, sew the short edges together and press the seam open. Turn the skirt right side out. Press the long folded edge to set the crease. Machine-baste the raw edges together.

7 For a pleated skirt, pin the raw edges of the skirt fabric to the cushion bottom piece. Pin the sides first, starting at the back and ending at the front corners. Then pin the front from the middle out. Fold in and pleat the excess evenly at the two front corners. Once you have determined the pleat position, unpin the skirt, lay it flat, and staple across the top edge to secure the pleat folds. Repin the skirt to the seat cover, right sides together. Machine-stitch, using a zipper foot to sew in close to the welt.

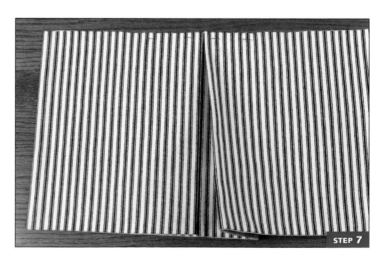

STEP 7

8 For a gathered skirt, set the machine for a wide, long zigzag stitch. Zigzag over thin, smooth string or dental floss along the raw edge just inside the machine basting. Pull up the string to gather the edge. Adjust the gathers to fit the cushion bottom piece, and pin in place. Machine-stitch, using a zipper foot to sew in close to the welt.

STEP 8

SCRAPS *of* Knowledge

ZIPPERS BY THE YARD

Zippers for home-dec use are sold by the yard, rather than in prepackaged lengths. You can find them at home-dec fabric stores or in a sewing notions catalog such as Clotilde®.

Nylon home-dec zippers are similar to the ones used in dresses and sell for about $6 per yard. Metal zippers are larger and clumsier to insert and cost about $1.50 per yard. Both zippers are strong, but the nylon zipper is worth the extra expense since it is softer and less visible.

The zipper tape you will purchase comes with many pulls on the spool. Be sure to tell the salesperson how many pulls you need. For example, if you were making three pillows that required 18 inches of zipper each, you would ask for 1½ yards of zipper and three pulls. Before you cut your purchased zipper tape into smaller lengths, make sure there is a zipper pull in the middle of each section. Bar-tack by hand or machine over the ends you want to stay closed, as the zipper tape does not include stops.

9 Fold the boxing strip in half crosswise, right side in, and sew the short ends together with a ½-inch seam allowance. Press the seam open. Pin the boxing strip to the cushion top, right sides together and with the seam at the back. Machine-stitch all around using a zipper foot. Repeat to join the cushion bottom, making sure the corners align. Stitch around three sides; leave the back edge open.

10 Fold each tie in half lengthwise, right side in. Machine-stitch ½ inch from the raw edge on one long and one short side. Clip the corner diagonally, turn right side out, and press. Tuck in the open end, and slipstitch closed. Tack the middle of each tie to the boxing strip to align with the chair stiles.

STEP 10

DESIGN IDEA For less noticeable ties, make narrow strips long enough to overlap when wrapped around the chair stiles. Attach Velcro hook-and-loop fasteners to the overlapping sections.

11 Fold the cushion in thirds and insert it into the cover through the opening. Slipstitch the opening closed.

WORKROOM TIP Place a foam cushion inside a plastic dry-cleaning bag before inserting it into a cushion cover. The plastic will glide against the fabric and counteract the sticking tendency of the foam. Remove the plastic before sewing the cushion cover closed.

WINDOW SEATS

Making a window seat is exactly like making boxed cushions for dining chairs (see p. 48). Tape pieces of newspaper together to make a sheet a little larger than the seating area, and use it to make a pattern. Take the pattern to the foam store, and ask to have a piece of 3- or 4-inch-thick foam cut to match it. They'll trace around the pattern to mark it on the foam. Make sure they cut inside the marked line or the foam will be too large for the window seat. If the angle is not too severe and the area is not too large, the cushion can be cut from one piece of foam. If this isn't possible, ask the foam shop to glue the pieces together permanently.

WORKROOM TIP When choosing fabric for a window seat, keep in mind that the sun will damage the fabric—you may want to add a coordinating window treatment above the seat.

The three examples that follow explain how to cut the fabric:

- Example I. If your fabric is solid, you can usually cut the cover by placing the foam lengthwise on the fabric. This is economical because you can fit the pieces close together.

- Example 2. If your fabric has a vertical print, you will need to align the foam across the fabric to maintain the orientation of the printed design. Because a window seat is usually wider than the fabric, you'll need to cut the top and bottom covers in several pieces. Don't place the seam in the center of the seat. Instead, use the full width of the fabric

for the center of the seat, and cut a smaller piece to go at each end to supplement the width.

- Example 3. When a printed fabric has a large repeat and you are cutting the cover in several pieces, you'll need extra fabric so you can match the pattern. How much you need depends on the size of the design repeat. Take the pattern to the store when you buy the fabric so you can see how much you'll need.

WORKROOM TIP Choose a contrasting fabric for the boxing so you won't have to match the print to the top cover.

Cutting the foam to the precise seat shape and dimensions produces a custom fit, as seen here. Welt in the seams accentuates the crisp lines.

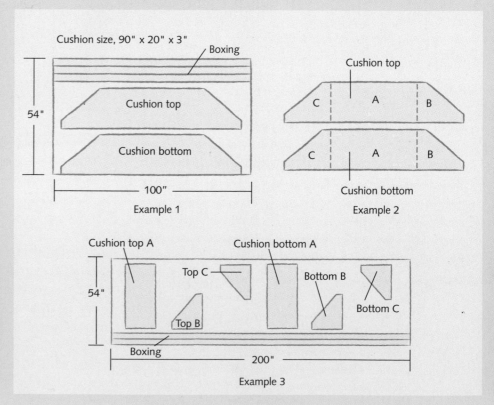

Example 1

Cushion size, 90" x 20" x 3"
Boxing
54"
Cushion top
Cushion bottom
100"

Example 2

Cushion top
C   A   B
C   A   B
Cushion bottom

Example 3

Cushion top A
Top C
Cushion bottom A
Bottom B
Bottom C
54"
Top B
Boxing
200"

Parsons Chair Slipcover

The simple lines of the Parsons chair are easy to work with, even if you've never sewn a slipcover before.

The Parsons chair is a modern silhouette that can change personalities as fast as you can change its slipcover. A tailored look can be achieved with a box pleated skirt; for a more feminine look, the skirt can be gathered. You'll need to decide where to put the opening: Will it be a zipper down the side or decorative buttons down the back? The complete design details are worked out with muslin fabric first, using the seamlines on the existing chair upholstery as a guide. Once you've made a slipcover for this easy shape, you're bound to see possibilities for reviving secondhand furniture that turns up at garage and estate sales.

Before You Begin see **Slipcover Fabric Yardages** on p. 56, **Fabric Preparation** on p. 94, **What Is Boxing?** on p. 50, **Single Welt** on p. 13, and **Sewing Zippers into Seams** on p. 172.

FOR EACH PARSONS CHAIR COVER, YOU'LL NEED:

- Fabric for chair cover
- Fabric and ¼-inch cord for welt
- Lining fabric for skirt
- Zipper
- Velcro hook-and-loop tape
- About 10 yards muslin
- Carpenter's level
- Measuring and marking tools
- General sewing/craft supplies

MAKING THE MUSLIN PATTERNS

1 Drape the muslin on the chair seat and backrest, letting it extend over the rolled back of the chair to the seamline. Fold a 3-inch tuck (an extra 6 inches of fabric) at the crevice where the seat and backrest meet. Trim off the excess muslin 3 inches beyond the existing upholstery's seat and backrest seamlines all around. Smooth the muslin in place, and pin close to the seamlines. Mark seamlines on the muslin using a dashed line. Unpin and remove the muslin chair seat/backrest, trim 1 inch beyond the dashed seamline all around, and repin the piece to the chair.

2 Cut a piece of muslin at least 3 inches larger all around than the side panel of the chair backrest. Smooth the muslin against this part of the chair, and pin from top to bottom and side to side at 4-inch to 6-inch intervals. Mark the seamline with a dashed line. Write "Cut 2" on the muslin piece, as a reminder to cut two pieces in mirror image, one for each side of the chair. Use a small ruler and a contrasting color to mark a 1½-inch flap along the back seam for the zipper closure. Unpin and remove the muslin side panel. Cut the flap along the marked line; then trim the remainder 1 inch beyond the marked seamline all around. Repin the piece to the chair.

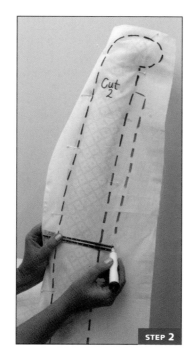

[WORKROOM TIP] Hold a carpenter's level perpendicular to the floor to mark the vertical grainline on each muslin piece. Add an arrowhead at each end of the line. Align the grainline parallel to the selvage edge of the decorator fabric to cut out the pieces.

3 Cut a piece of muslin at least 3 inches larger all around than the chair back. This piece can extend all the way to the floor, to include a skirt, or it can stop earlier, at the top of the skirt, as shown in our design. Fold down the top edge of the muslin 1 inch. Align the fold on the seam where the rolled curve meets the back, and pin in place. Continue pinning down each side at 4-inch to 6-inch intervals. Mark the side seamlines. Add a 1½-inch flap for the side closure on one edge, to correspond to the flap on the side panel.

4 Label all three muslin pieces, and mark arrows to indicate the fabric grain. Also add notches (A, B, C, etc.) along the seamlines for matching up later. Unpin and remove the muslin back panel. Trim 1 inch beyond the side edges only (the bottom edge will be marked and cut later), and repin the piece to the chair.

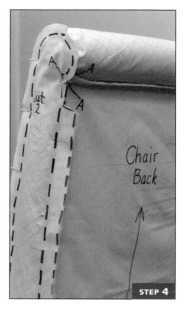

[WORKROOM TIP] Use pieces of muslin to work out features and details not present on the original chair, such as a boxing strip around the seat or a pleated or gathered skirt. Allow 12 inches of extra fabric for each box pleat. Allow 2½ times the boxing strip measurement for a gathered skirt.

5 To design the boxing, cut a wide strip of muslin to fit around the edge of the seat sides and front plus 6 inches. Use a straightedge to mark a dashed line 1 inch in from one long edge for the skirt seam. Pin the opposite long edge to the muslin seat, making the boxing as shallow or as deep as you like; it does not have to match the depth of the chair seat. Pin the ends to the muslin back panel. Use a carpenter's level to check that the skirt seamline is level all around, and adjust the pins as needed.

6 Extend the skirt seamline across the muslin back panel, from edge to edge. Trim off the excess muslin 1 inch below the marked line, so that the boxing strip and back panel are even. Mark the seat seamline on the muslin boxing strip. Unpin the strip, and trim 1 inch beyond the seat seamline. Label the boxing strip.

7 Unpin the remaining muslin pieces. Set the machine for a long basting stitch. With contrasting thread, sew the muslin pieces together along the marked seamlines, matching the notches where indicated; leave the tab closure open. Put the muslin cover on the chair inside out to test the fit, and adjust the seams as needed. Do not remove the muslin from the chair.

8 To measure for the skirt, run a tape measure once around the chair—sides, front, and back—at the boxing strip level (A). Also measure the distance from the skirt seamline to the floor or to the desired finished hem length (B). Measure B in several places to confirm that the skirt will hang uniformly all around. Measure each seam that you plan to trim with welt, and add an extra 2 inches for each join or seam (C). Jot down your figures for A, B, and C.

[WORKROOM TIP] Let the weight of the fabric determine the hem style. A 4-inch double-fold hem is standard on draperies, but for slipcovers you can serge the edge and fold up once 2 inches from the edge. Pleated corners do not hang well with a lot of bulk. Instead of hemming the lower edge, you might consider binding it with contrasting fabric. For professional results, make one or more sample hems to try out your ideas.

9 For a lined skirt with a bound hem and box pleats at the corners, cut a muslin rectangle that measures A plus 48 inches (four pleats at 12 inches each) by B plus 1 inch. Pin

TRICK
of the TRADE

MAKING SLIPCOVER PATTERNS WITH MUSLIN

Follow these pointers to make your muslin slipcover patterns fit perfectly.

- Use batting to pad and smooth over tufting, channels, or buttons in the original upholstery. A few layers may be necessary. Tack the batting to the chair by hand before introducing the muslin.

- Remove the seat cushion to fit the muslin for the inside back and the base of the seat, or deck. Where the chair

arms, deck, and inside back meet, tuck in the muslin as far as it will go for plenty of allowance.

- Use a marker or pencil to mark the seamlines on the muslin. Follow the seamlines on the existing upholstery or introduce new lines, if you're feeling adventurous. Use a level to mark a straight grainline. Mark an arrow to indicate the fabric direction.

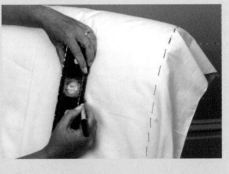

- As you add more muslin pieces, label each piece. The shapes will look different once they are disassembled and laid flat, and labeling will prevent confusion. Also mark and label key matching points or notches on the seamlines so that you know how to sew the pieces together.

the muslin skirt to the back panel, leaving ½ inch free at the closure edge. When you reach the first corner, fold a box pleat 3 inches deep, using up 12 inches of fabric. Continue pinning the muslin skirt to the boxing strip all around. When you reach the remaining back corner, fold a 3-inch pleat (using 6 inches of fabric) along the side panel. Allow for a 3-inch flap to go around the corner, and trim off the excess. Use a marking pen to mark all the pleat folds on the muslin.

10 Remove the muslin cover from the chair, take out all the seam stitching, and trim the seam allowances to ½ inch. Use the muslin pattern pieces to determine how much fabric you will need. Buy welt cord and enough contrasting fabric to make a welt to length C. Buy a zipper the same length as the side closure flap.

DESIGN IDEA Combine several fabrics for a more interesting slipcover. The project shown uses toile for the seat and backrest; a check for the boxing strip, side panels, and hem trim; and a stripe for the skirt, back, and welt.

MAKING THE SLIPCOVER

1 Prepare the fabrics for sewing. Use the muslin patterns to cut out the fabric pieces you will need. Include flaps for the zipper closure along one back seam only. If you need to join pieces of fabric together for the skirt, cut the pieces so that the seams will be hidden in the pleat folds. For the hem binding, cut a 3⅜-inch-wide strip, piecing as needed to make one piece that measures A plus 48 inches.

2 Make the covered welt, allowing for a ½-inch lip. Pin and sew the welt to the appropriate fabric pieces, as determined earlier. In the project shown, welt was sewn around each side panel; around the chair seat, up to the 6-inch tuck allowance; and across the lower edge of the back.

WORKROOM TIP If you use decorative cord instead of welt, be sure to purchase one continuous piece to go around the main pattern pieces. Watch closely as the cord is measured at the fabric store.

SCRAPS *of* Knowledge

SLIPCOVER FABRIC YARDAGES

The best way to determine how much fabric you will need for a slipcover is to make muslin patterns and take them with you to the store. Fabrics with large pattern repeats can gobble up a lot of yardage, especially if you are covering a group of chairs. By placing the muslin patterns directly on the fabric, you can determine how much extra fabric will be needed to match patterns or plaids. If you do a lot of home-dec projects, you might want to purchase muslin by the bolt to have on hand for making patterns. Sample yardages are shown at right.

SAMPLE SLIPCOVER YARDAGES

Furniture	Fabric for Slipcover*	Fabric for Welt*
Parsons chair	Up to 6 yards	1¼ yards
Wing chair	Up to 9 yards	1½ yards
Loveseat with 4 loose cushions	Up to 15 yards	2 yards
Full sofa with 6 loose cushions	Up to 23 yards	2½ yards

* Yardages listed are for fabrics 54 inches to 60 inches wide. Increase the listed yardage by 30 percent for fabrics 36 inches to 45 inches wide. Allow extra to match pattern repeats. Increase the listed yardage by 10 percent for a loose, baggy, "shabby chic" look.

3 Join a side panel to the back panel, installing a zipper along the flap edge. The zipper does not go into the skirt.

4 Place the backrest/seat panel on the back panel, right sides together and top edges matching. Machine-stitch ½ inch from the edge (this is the seam that falls at the inside of the rolled top). Starting at the zipper, continue pinning the side panel to this larger piece, right sides together and matching the labeled notches. Pin the other side panel to the piece in the same way. Machine-stitch with a ½-inch seam allowance, stopping ½ inch from the end of the side panel on the seat side.

5 Pin the boxing strip to the seat, right sides together. Start at the middle of the front edge of the seat and work out toward each side, stopping when you reach the 6-inch tuck allowance at the back of the seat. Pin the remainder of the strip to the lower edge of the side panel on each side. Stitch the boxing strip in place, keeping the tuck allowance loose. Stitch the end of the boxing strip to the back panel on the side without the zipper; leave the other end free.

6 Sew the skirt pieces together to make a piece the appropriate size (as determined in the previous section, step 9). Cut and sew a lining to match. Trim ½ inch off the lining at both ends. Place the skirt and lining right sides together, and stitch the shorter edges together. Trim the seam allowances to ¼ inch. Turn right side out and press, allowing the skirt fabric to fold ¼ inch toward the lining side. Sew the raw edges together. Bind the lower raw edge with the contrasting strip cut in step 1.

7 Pin the skirt to the boxing strip and back panel and form the pleats at the corners. Staple the top edge to temporarily hold the pleats in place. Sew the skirt to the boxing strip. Turn in the top edges of the flap at the end and sew by hand.

8 Turn the slipcover right side out, put it on the chair, and close the zipper. Attach Velcro hook-and-loop tape to hold the boxing strip and flap closed below the zipper. Fold the tuck allowance and push it into the crevice between the seat and backrest.

[WORKROOM TIP] If you prewashed your fabric, then your slipcover can be washed and dried by machine whenever necessary. Close the zipper during laundering so the teeth don't rub against the inside seams. For a smooth fit, pull the cover out of the dryer when it is still slightly damp and slip it over the chair to finish drying.

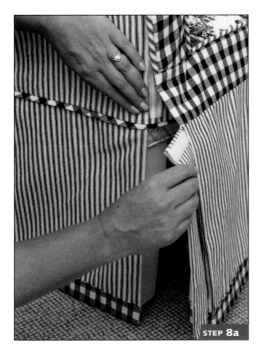

STEP 8a

STEP 8b

STEP 8c

Part 3

SLEEPING COMFORT

Your bedroom is your personal retreat from the busyness of life. Make this room soft and inviting. Cover your bed with a luxurious down or silk comforter and pile on beautiful pillows for a place you can't wait to return to at the end of the day. Covering the walls with fabric will make the room warmer and more intimate as well as add a measure of soundproofing. Decorate your sheets and pillowcases with machine embroidery, make a fabric-covered headboard, or sew a sheer canopy for the bed. Everything about this room can be beautiful, and you can create it all.

Duvet Cover

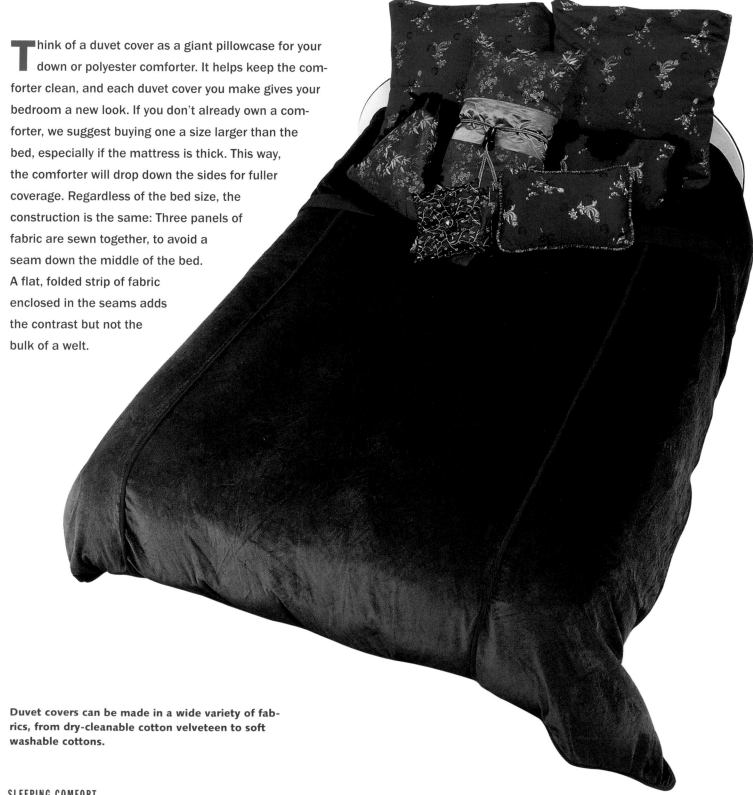

Think of a duvet cover as a giant pillowcase for your down or polyester comforter. It helps keep the comforter clean, and each duvet cover you make gives your bedroom a new look. If you don't already own a comforter, we suggest buying one a size larger than the bed, especially if the mattress is thick. This way, the comforter will drop down the sides for fuller coverage. Regardless of the bed size, the construction is the same: Three panels of fabric are sewn together, to avoid a seam down the middle of the bed. A flat, folded strip of fabric enclosed in the seams adds the contrast but not the bulk of a welt.

Duvet covers can be made in a wide variety of fabrics, from dry-cleanable cotton velveteen to soft washable cottons.

Before You Begin ▊ see **Fabric Preparation** on p. 94.

FOR ONE DUVET COVER, YOU'LL NEED:

- Comforter
- Fabric, at least 44 inches wide
- Zipper
- Decorative buttons
- 2 yards twill tape
- Measuring and marking tools
- General craft/sewing supplies

PLANNING THE PROJECT

1 Use the worksheet on p. 63 to measure your comforter and figure out the fabric yardage needed. Be sure to measure the fabric width itself, since the information on the bolt may not be accurate. To make a duvet cover for an 89-inch by 95-inch queen-size comforter in a plain fabric, allowing extra for shrinkage, we used 5⅜ yards of 54-inch-wide fabric for each side, or 10¾ yards total.

2 Purchase your fabric. You can use the same fabric for both sides of the cover or two contrasting fabrics, one on each side, for a different look when the comforter is flipped over. Also purchase a zipper 6 inches shorter than A on the worksheet. Also plan now for the decorative flap; if this piece cannot be cut from your leftover fabric, you will need to buy additional fabric for it.

STEP 2

DESIGN IDEA Flat sheets can be used for one or both sides of the duvet cover instead of fabric. Using sheets eliminates the need to sew fabric panels together. For a proper fit, the sheet must measure at least 1½ inches larger than the comforter all around after preshrinking. Sheet sizes are listed on the package.

SCRAPS of Knowledge

FEATHER-AND-DOWN COMFORTERS

High-quality feather-and-down comforters use a baffle box construction for the maximum feather loft. Unlike quilting, which brings the top and bottom layers of fabric closer together, baffles are three-dimensional channels within the top and bottom fabrics that allow the feathers to move about and expand. The loft determines both the weight and the warmth of the comforter. A loft weight of 750 is warmer, puffier, and weighs more than a loft weight of 450. Any weight above 650 is considered luxury weight.

Another sign of comforter quality is in the fabric covering, or ticking. Ticking should be 100 percent cotton with a 200-count weave or higher to prevent small feathers from escaping. Seams should be double-sewn, not serged, for the same reason. This is true for the ticking on pillow forms as well. For more information on feathers and down, see p. 175.

Perhaps you are allergic to feathers? Silk gives the same luxurious feel and light hand of feathers and down but is softer and more flexible, allowing the comforter to conform to the body. Silk-filled comforters also come in different weights. See Resources on p. 198 for more information.

3 Prepare the fabric for sewing by preshrinking it, cutting off the selvages, and straightening the ends.

MAKING THE FRONT AND BACK

1 Cut the fabric for the duvet front cover from selvage to selvage, referring to E on the worksheet for the panel length and F for the number of panels to cut (either two or three). Mark the top of each panel on the wrong side with a piece of tape. Arrange the panels side by side, with one panel in the middle. If you have only two panels, cut one panel in half lengthwise to make two side panels, and place one on either side of the large panel to avoid a seam down the middle. Mark the inside cut edges for seaming to the center panel later.

2 For the seam trim, cut two contrasting strips of fabric, each 1¾ inches by the length of one panel, piecing as necessary. Press each strip in half lengthwise, right side in. Pin each strip to a long edge of the center panel, raw edges matching. Machine-baste ½ inch from the edge.

STEP 2

3 Pin the side panels to the center panel, right sides together, as planned in step 1. Observe your tape markings, to make sure napped panels all run in the same direction. Line up any patterns across the seam. With the center panel on top, machine-stitch on the basting line through all layers, trapping the trim in the seam. Press the seams in the opposite direction of the contrasting strip.

4 Spread the front cover on the floor. Measure across the joined panels, from edge to edge. Jot down your measurement, subtract A, and divide by 2. Trim each side panel by this amount so that the width across is now A, or 3 inches wider than the comforter. Measure to confirm that the length is B, or 3 inches longer than the comforter, and trim as needed.

[WORKROOM TIP] For a fuller, more puffy appearance on the bed, cut the pieces for the front and back cover to match the comforter dimensions instead of 3 inches larger.

5 Repeat steps 1–4 to make the back cover.

6 For a decorative accent, use leftover fabric or another fabric to make a flap. Cut a strip that measures 9 inches wide by A. Fold it in half lengthwise, wrong side in, and press to set the crease. Lay the front cover right side up on a flat surface. Lay the strip straight across the cover, side edges matching and the fold 15½ inches from the top edge. Machine-stitch along the raw edge with a ½-inch seam allowance. Trim the seam allowance to ¼ inch. Fold the flap down onto the cover to hide the seam. Sew decorative buttons evenly spaced across the flap to hold it in place.

STEP 6

INSTALLING THE ZIPPER

1 Lay the front cover right side up on a flat surface. Center the zipper along the bottom edge of the cover, right sides together and edges matching. Machine-stitch ¼ inch from the edge.

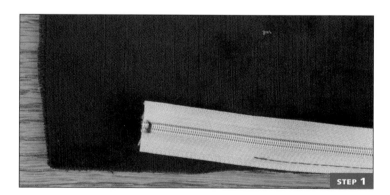

STEP 1

2 Repeat step 1 to sew the other edge of the zipper tape to the lower edge of the back cover.

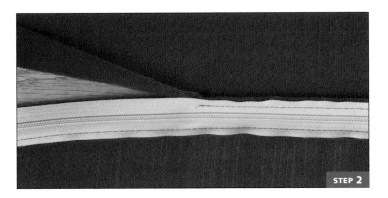

STEP 2

3 To hide the zipper, fold the fabric back on itself, wrong side in, ¾ inch from the zipper tape, for a self-flap.

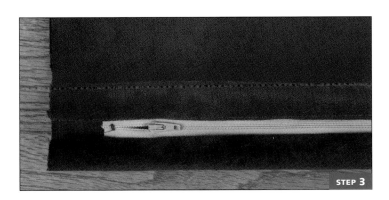

STEP 3

4 Topstitch through two layers, close to the zipper teeth, to hold the flap in place.

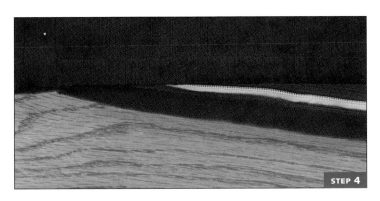

STEP 4

DESIGN IDEA A zipper is just one way to close the bottom edge. Create your own closure design using buttons, ties, snaps, or Velcro hook-and-loop fastener.

ASSEMBLING THE DUVET COVER

1 Open the zipper partway. Pin the front and back covers right sides together and edges matching. Machine-stitch ½ inch from the edge all around, right up to the zipper closure. Trim the corners diagonally to reduce bulk.

2 Cut eight 8-inch lengths of twill tape to use as ties. Sew one tie to the seam allowance by each corner of the duvet cover. Sew a corresponding tie to each corner of the comforter. Lay the cover, still wrong side out, on the bed. Open the zipper all the way. Arrange the comforter on top and tie together at the corners. Turn the cover right side out, enclosing the comforter inside. Adjust the fullness and zip closed.

DESIGN IDEA Enclose a contrasting welt in the outside seam of a comforter cover. You may want to omit the welt along the top edge to keep it soft and comfortable against your face while you are sleeping.

DUVET COVER WORKSHEET

Jot down measurements A, B, C, and D in inches. Then do the calculations.

Comforter width, plus 3"	(A)_____
Comforter length, plus 3"	(B)_____
Fabric width, minus 4"	(C)_____
Pattern repeat, if any	(D)_____
Add B plus D, for the cut-panel length.	(E)_____
Divide A by C, and round up to the nearest whole number. This is the number of fabric widths required.	(F)_____
Multiply E times F.	(G)_____

Divide G by 36"; this is the required fabric yardage for *one side of the duvet cover.* Add ½ yard extra if you will be preshrinking the fabric.

_____ yards fabric

Bed Skirt

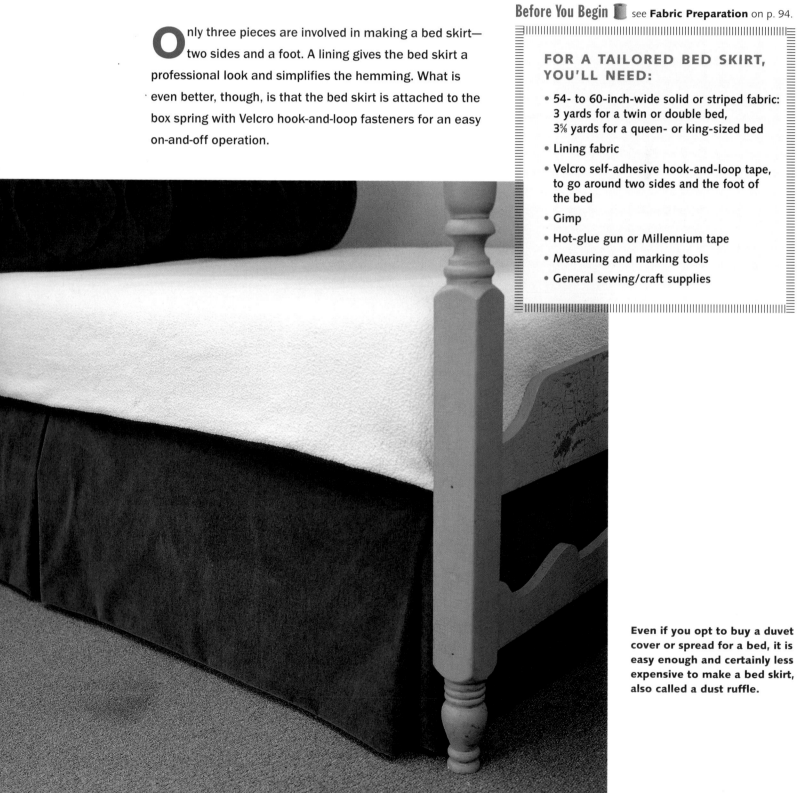

Only three pieces are involved in making a bed skirt—two sides and a foot. A lining gives the bed skirt a professional look and simplifies the hemming. What is even better, though, is that the bed skirt is attached to the box spring with Velcro hook-and-loop fasteners for an easy on-and-off operation.

Before You Begin see **Fabric Preparation** on p. 94.

FOR A TAILORED BED SKIRT, YOU'LL NEED:

- 54- to 60-inch-wide solid or striped fabric: 3 yards for a twin or double bed, 3⅜ yards for a queen- or king-sized bed
- Lining fabric
- Velcro self-adhesive hook-and-loop tape, to go around two sides and the foot of the bed
- Gimp
- Hot-glue gun or Millennium tape
- Measuring and marking tools
- General sewing/craft supplies

Even if you opt to buy a duvet cover or spread for a bed, it is easy enough and certainly less expensive to make a bed skirt, also called a dust ruffle.

SEWING THE BED SKIRT PANELS

1 Using a hot-glue gun or Millennium tape, affix Velcro "loop" tape to the top outer edge of the box spring, just under the welted seam. Use one continuous strip to go around the sides and foot of the bed.

STEP 1

2 Measure the length of the box spring for measurement A and the width of the box spring for measurement B. For the depth (measurement C), measure down from the top edge of the Velcro tape to ½ inch above the floor. Jot down your figures for A, B, and C.

3 Prepare the fabrics for sewing by preshrinking them, cutting off the selvages, and straightening the ends.

4 Measure C plus 3½ inches from one cut end of the fabric, and mark a line across the fabric width. Cut on the marked line for one panel. Repeat to cut five panels total for a double or twin bed and six panels for a queen or king bed. Cut the same number of panels from the lining fabric, making each one C minus 2½ inches deep.

[WORKROOM TIP] Drapery lining comes in white and off-white and is relatively inexpensive to purchase. If you keep 10 yards or so of drapery lining on hand, you won't have to make a special trip to the store every time a project idea hits you. You'll also be less tempted to omit the lining on a project that really should have one.

5 Seam the fabric panels together in pairs along one short edge. Each two-panel section will cover one side or foot of the bed; the exception is the twin or double bed, where one panel will be used at the foot. Seam the lining panels the same way. Press the seams open.

6 Place the fabric and lining pieces right sides together, bottom edges matching, and sew with a ½-inch seam allowance. Press the seam toward the lining.

STEP 6

7 Fold the work in half, wrong side in and edges matching. Machine-baste the top edges together. Serge-finish the side edges. Fold in each side edge 2 inches, and machine-stitch in place. Press to set the crease at the lower edge, forming a self-hem.

STEP 7

ATTACHING THE SKIRT TO THE BOX SPRING

1 Mark the midpoint of one side of the bed by inserting a straight pin into the Velcro tape. Starting at the head of the bed, pin the bed skirt to the box spring. When you reach the midpoint, fold a box pleat at least 3 inches deep on each side. Hide the center seam behind the pleat fold that is closer to the foot of the bed. Continue pinning down to the foot of the bed. Make a single pleat at the foot of the bed, and let the end extend about 1 inch around the corner to hide the bed frame. Adjust the pleats as needed so the fabric is distributed evenly along the length of the box spring.

STEP 2

STEP 1

2 Repeat step 1 to pin the bed skirt to the foot and remaining side of the box spring. The skirt at the foot of a twin or double bed will not have a center seam; simply form the pleat at the middle. At the foot of the bed, overlap the 1-inch extensions and secure with a safety pin. Also pin the pleat layers together.

3 Unpin the entire bed skirt from the box spring. It will be quite heavy and awkward to handle; make sure the safety pins continue to hold the pleats securely. At the machine, fold the pleats flat, with the bottom edges even. Machine-stitch each pleat along the top edge to hold the folds in place. Also stitch the end pleats and corner overlaps.

4 Hand-walk the bed skirt around the Velcro tape on the box spring. If it is not fitting perfectly, adjust and restitch the corner overlaps. Serge the top raw edge. Hot-glue the Velcro "hook" tape to the wrong side, along the top edge. Hot-glue gimp or decorative braid around the top edge to conceal the serging. Attach the bed skirt to the box spring.

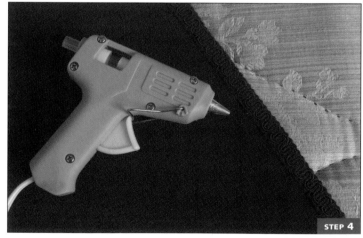

STEP 4

DESIGN IDEA For a softer look, gather the edge of the bed skirt. Make a skirt 2½ times wider than each side of the bed. Gather onto a 1-inch-wide ribbon. See Gathering on p. 49 for more information.

Windowpane Bed Canopy

||||||||||||||||||||||||||||||||||||||||||||||||

**FOR ONE BED CANOPY,
YOU'LL NEED:**

- 118-inch-wide sheer drapery fabric: 5 yards
  for double or queen-size bed, 7 yards for
  king- or California king–size bed
- Hardwood slats
- Fabric leaves, herbs, dried flowers, etc.
- 2⅝-inch-wide ribbon
- Glue
- Fasturn® tool
- Drill
- 70/10 HJ or HM machine needle
- Measuring and marking tools
- General sewing/craft supplies

||||||||||||||||||||||||||||||||||||||||||||||||

If you have a high four-poster bed, you can turn it into a unique canopied retreat. The canopy is supported by wooden slats that run from post to post. Overhead, fabric leaves from Pottery Barn are suspended between two sheer panels. You can fill the windowpanes on your canopy with anything you like, from lavender to dried flowers.

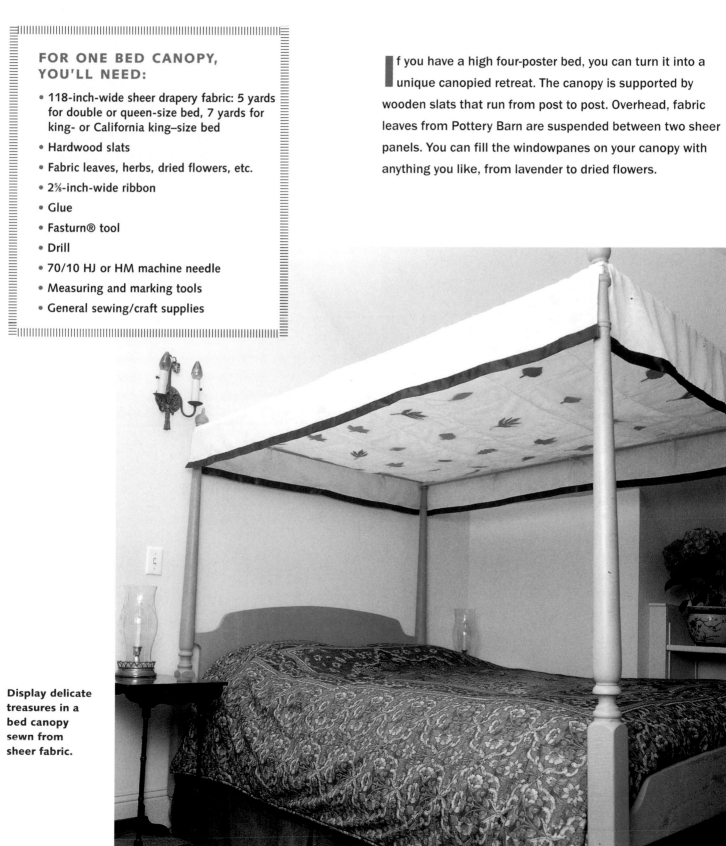

Display delicate treasures in a bed canopy sewn from sheer fabric.

MAKING THE CANOPY FRAME

1 Measure the bed length (for measurement A) and width (measurement B) from post to post. Jot down your figures for A and B. Purchase two hardwood slats for each measurement.

2 Remove the finial from each post. Drill a hole in the end of each slat to fit over the bedpost screws or pegs. Then replace the finials to hold the slats in place.

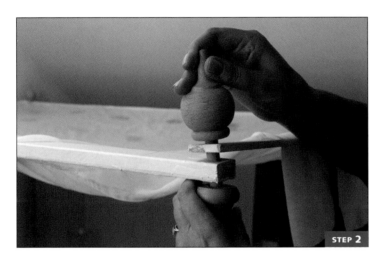

STEP 2

SEWING THE WINDOWPANES

1 Trim off the selvages from the 118-inch-wide sheer fabric. Cut a double layer of sheer fabric 1 inch larger all around than your A by B dimensions.

2 To work out a grid for the canopy top, use a calculator to divide A and B into equal sections. For example, if your canopy measures 48 inches by 60 inches, you might end up with a 6 by 6 grid, with each block measuring 8 inches by 10 inches—a nice size for displaying your treasures.

3 Use a pencil and ruler to lightly mark the gridlines on one of the sheer panels, remembering to allow 1 inch extra all around for seaming the overhang. Place one of your treasures in the middle of each frame.

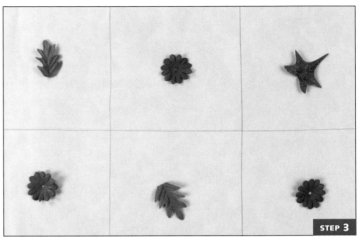

STEP 3

4 Move the treasures around until you are happy with their placement. Lift up each treasure, put a few dots of glue on the back, and reposition on the fabric. The glued side will face the ceiling, so don't worry if the glue shows. Overlay the second piece of sheer fabric, sandwiching the treasures inside. Pin the layers together, using two pins in each frame. Avoid pinning on the pencil lines.

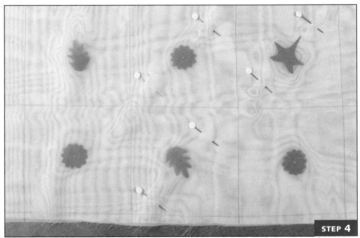

STEP 4

5 Fit the sewing machine with a new sharp fine needle, 70/10 HJ or HM. Machine-stitch along the marked gridlines, which will be visible through the top sheer layer. Sew all the vertical lines first, and then sew across horizontally, locking each treasure in its pocket. Finish by stitching 1 inch from the edge all around. Insert a pin somewhere in this top layer to mark it as the "right" side, or the side that will face the bed. Don't worry if a treasure shifts in its box. You can anchor it down later with a hand stitch.

ASSEMBLING THE CANOPY

1 Cut the pieces for the overhang, or drop, from the remaining sheer fabric. For the side drops, cut two pieces 1 inch longer than A and 18 inches wide. For the end drops, at the head and foot of the bed, cut two pieces 1 inch longer than B and 18 inches wide.

2 Fold each drop in half lengthwise, right side in. Serge the short ends together ½ inch from the edge, letting the serger cut off ½ inch. Turn right side out and press.

3 To accent each drop, cut a piece of 2⅜-inch-wide ribbon 1 inch longer than the folded edge. Press the ribbon in half lengthwise. Fold each cut end ½ inch to the inside and finger-press. Enclose the ribbon around the folded edge by ⅜ inch. Topstitch in place through all layers.

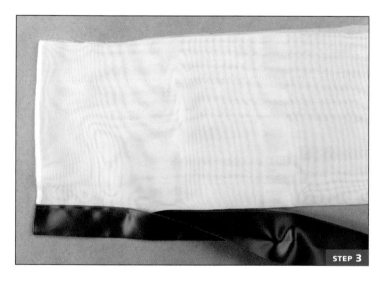

4 For the ties, cut five 1¼-inch by 36-inch-long strips from the sheer fabric. Fold each strip in half lengthwise. Using a three-thread serger and a narrow serger stitch, serge off ⅛ inch. Use Fasturn to turn each tube right side out. Cut each piece in half to make ten 18-inch-long ties.

5 Remove the canopy frame, if possible, and place it on the floor. Lay the canopy top on it, centered, and trace ¼ inch beyond the outer edge of the frame. Trim off any excess beyond this line. Mark and stitch a diagonal buttonhole at each corner to fit over the finial screw or peg.

6 Pin the drops to the wrong side of the canopy top, matching the edges on each side. Fold each tie in half and pin the folded edge in the seam evenly spaced along the edge, two at each end and three on the sides. Sew (do not serge) with ½-inch seams, catching the ties in the seam as you go.

7 Lay the canopy on the frame. The seam should fall ¼ inch inside the edge of the frame at each end, so that it will be hidden from view when mounted. Adjust as needed. Serge the four seams, cutting off ¼ inch. Sew a Velcro hook-and-loop circle to the large panel near each tie. Glue the Velcro mate to the canopy frame.

8 Tie the canopy onto the frame, and press the Velcro fasteners together. Remount the frame on the bedposts, inserting the screws through the buttonholes.

Machine-Embroidered Linens

If you like machine embroidery but are ready to move beyond T-shirts, home-dec sewing may be the perfect outlet. Sheets, pillowcases, and towels await your special touch. With such a wide array of fabric stabilizers available in today's market, there is scarcely a fabric that cannot be embroidered. The key to a professional look is using the right stabilizer, the right thread, and the right needle.

Machine embroidery can be applied to purchased linens, such as flannel sheets, pillowcases, and towels.

Before You Begin see **Machine-Embroidery Equipment** on p. 72.

FOR MACHINE EMBROIDERY, YOU'LL NEED:

- Purchased item or fabric to embroider
- Decorative thread
- Bobbin thread
- Sewing machine with embroidery capabilities
- Metafil/Metallica needle size 80/12 HE
- SdSV™ or dSV™ stabilizer
- Sulky KK 2000 Temporary Spray Adhesive
- Measuring and marking tools
- General sewing/craft supplies

PREPARING THE MATERIAL

1 Select a design for embroidery, and determine the size and placement on the screen of your machine. Some high-end machines can change the size of the design. Set up your machine with a Metafil needle and appropriate bobbin and upper threads.

[WORKROOM TIP] Before you stitch on your actual project, do a test piece using the same needle, threads, fabric, and stabilizers to work out any problems. If you are stitching on a purchased item, such as a pillowcase, choose a similar fabric for testing.

2 Determine the location on your fabric or project material for your embroidered design. Use chalk or a disappearing marker to mark the center point of the design as well as the boundaries.

3 Draw horizontal and vertical lines on the fabric through the center of the design. Hoops have corresponding marks on the edges that you can use to line up the work.

EMBROIDERING BY MACHINE

1 Make the embroidery sandwich by placing the fabric between two sheets of stabilizer. For the bottom layer, you might use SdSV stabilizer, pressing the sticky side against the wrong side of the fabric. For the top layer, you might spray the fabric surface with Sulky KK 2000 and overlay a sheet of dSV stabilizer. Hoop all three layers together, using the alignment marks made earlier and following the manufacturer's instructions.

[WORKROOM TIP] Items such as terry-cloth towels are too bulky to hoop. In this case, peel off the backing from SdSV, lay the hoop and fabric on top, and press down so they both adhere. Top with a few layers of dSV to keep the loops of the terry flat as you work the embroidery.

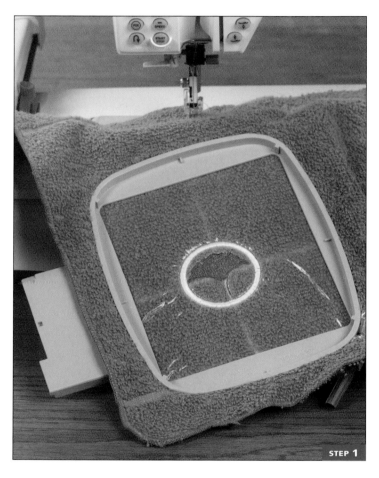

STEP 1

2 Set the work on the machine bed, and begin stitching your design. Trim the threads between color changes. When the embroidery is completed, remove the work from the machine. Tear away the stabilizer. It may be necessary to immerse your project in cool water to get rid of all markings and stabilizer.

DESIGN IDEA Check your button collection for terrific buttons that you can use along with your embroidery designs.

MACHINE-EMBROIDERY EQUIPMENT

Having and using the right tools will go a long way to ensuring your machine embroidery success. Here are some pointers to help you along.

Needles

- Use the Metafil/Metallica needle size 80/12 HE. It works with almost any thread or fabric. Use size 70/10 HE, which makes a smaller hole, on batiste, organza, and fine silks.

- Change needles often. Because machine-embroidery stitching is so dense, the needle dulls much more rapidly than in seam sewing. A popping or snapping sound signals a dull needle; so do snags in the fabric and skipped stitches. If you are working on a large design, you may need to change the needle between colors.

Thread

- For a high sheen, use rayon thread on top. Solid, twist, and variegated threads are available. A 30-weight to 35-weight thread gives fuller coverage, but if your machine can't handle the thicker thread, use 40-weight instead. Rayon thread is hand-washable and can be pressed with a warm iron on the synthetics setting. It is a good choice for decorative items but not items that require frequent washing, such as napkins, pillowcases, and towels.

- For all-around versatility, use polyester thread. It has a slight sheen, is colorfast, and can be machine-laundered or dry-cleaned. It also has a slight amount of stretch, making it suitable for knits or anything you plan to launder a lot.

- For embroidery on linen or cotton, use cotton thread. These fabrics require high heat for a crisp press, something cotton thread can handle. Cotton thread washes well but will fade with time. It has a flat, matte finish.

- For a novelty look, try silk or metallic threads. Silk thread is very fine and does not provide the best coverage, but it is useful for accents. Metallic-thread embroidery is dramatic to look at but scratchy to the touch. The most supple and strongest of the metallic threads is called Yenmet, available from Oklahoma Embroidery Supply. Both silk and metallic thread are washable in cold water only and must be line-dried or tumble-dried on low heat.

- For children's items, have fun with solar thread. This off-white thread turns to vivid hues when exposed to sunlight.

- Use a lightweight bobbin thread in black or white, such as The Finishing Touch® or Robison-Anton, to prevent thread buildup under your design. If the underside of the embroidery will be seen and you'd prefer a colored thread, try DMC® heirloom cotton 60-weight thread. Serger thread, while lightweight, is not recommended.

Stabilizers

- Sandwich the fabric between two stabilizer sheets to prevent twisting and distortion as you embroider.

- The biggest hassle about stabilizers is getting them off from the fabric and clear of the stitching after the design is completed. A good water-soluble stabilizer is dSV—simply run the finished item through a cold-water rinse cycle to dissolve it completely. A good tearaway stabilizer is Totally Stable™ by Sulky. This iron-on stabilizer has a waxy side that can be pressed against the wrong side of the fabric. Totally Stable on the bottom of the sandwich and dSV on the top make a useful pairing for many projects.

- To help hold the stabilizer in place, spray Sulky KK 2000 onto the fabric top and bottom before sandwiching the layers together. Some stabilizers already have a sticky surface on them. One of these is SdSV, a relative of dSV.

- To embroider sheer fabrics, make the sandwich with polyester mesh on the underside and dSV on the top. Polyester mesh is lightweight and has some drape.

Fabric-Covered Headboard

Take a plain bed and go seriously upscale with the addition of a covered headboard. A headboard always makes a bed look more permanent and cozy. This headboard is built with Homasote® board, available at lumberyards and home improvement centers. It is easy to cut, so you can make any shape headboard you like. Home decorating magazines are good resources for ideas.

Before You Begin 🧵 see **Foam Cushions** on p. 45.

FOR ONE HEADBOARD, YOU'LL NEED:

- Decorator fabric
- Lining fabric
- 4-foot by 8-foot Homasote fiberboard
- 2-inch-thick foam
- 3 yards to 4 yards 1-inch-thick upholstery batting
- Gimp
- Spray adhesive
- Small pruning saw
- Measuring and marking tools
- General sewing/craft supplies

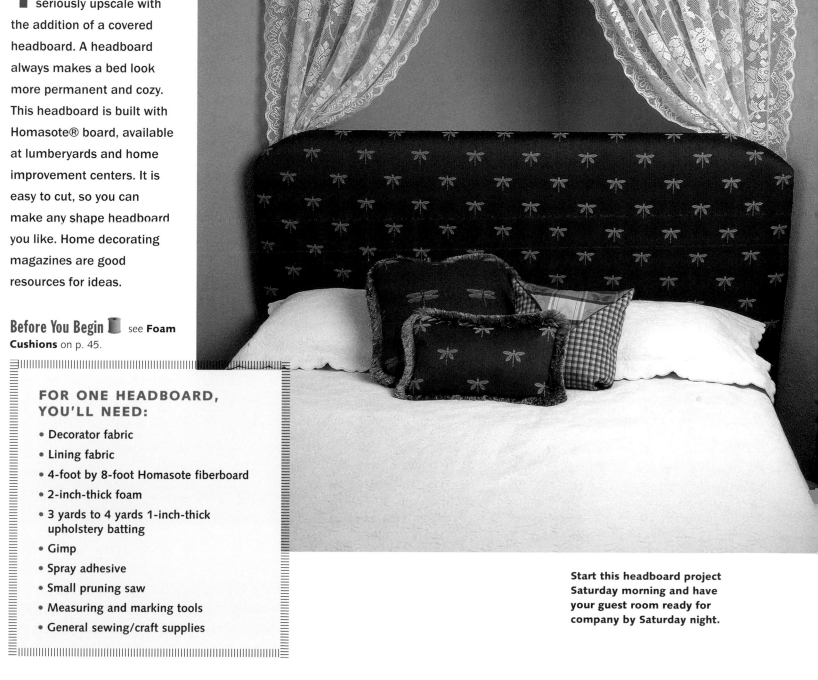

Start this headboard project Saturday morning and have your guest room ready for company by Saturday night.

PLANNING THE PROJECT

1 Measure across the bed frame from side to side and add 2 inches to determine the headboard length. Decide on a height for the headboard, up to 48 inches or the width of one Homasote fiberboard. (For a taller headboard, see the sidebar on the facing page.) Draw your headboard dimensions directly onto a 4-foot by 8-foot Homasote panel.

2 To shape the top edge, make an actual-size paper pattern on sheets of newspaper taped together. Fold the paper in half to cut out the shape and to make it symmetrical. Tape the pattern to the Homasote board and trace the edge. Cut the board on the marked lines with a small pruning saw to make the headboard frame.

3 Measure across the frame and add 6 inches, for measurement A. Measure the frame height and add 6 inches, for measurement B. Jot down your figures. If A is less than the width of the fabric, then simply purchase yardage that is equivalent to B. If A exceeds your fabric width, then you will have to piece the fabric together to get the required length. In this case, purchase yardage equivalent to 2 times B. If the fabric has a pattern repeat, up the yardage by the amount of the pattern repeat. Another option is to railroad the fabric, or cut it with A along the lengthwise rather than the crosswise grain. Railroading is not possible with fabrics that have an obvious up-and-down design. Figure out the yardage requirements for your headboard frame. You will also need drapery lining, 2-inch-thick upholstery foam, and 1-inch-thick batting the same size as the frame and gimp to go around it.

ASSEMBLING THE HEADBOARD

1 Use the headboard frame as a template to cut the same shape from the lining fabric, batting, and foam. Use spray adhesive to affix the foam to the frame. Then affix the batting to the foam. Set the lining piece aside.

2 Cut the fabric to measure A by B. If necessary, seam pieces of fabric together to obtain this size. Two seams joining three panels will be more attractive than one seam down the middle. Press the fabric well to eliminate all wrinkles.

3 Lay the fabric facedown on a flat work surface. Center the frame on top, padded side down.

STEP 3

4 Pin the edges of the fabric loosely to the sides of the foam. Turn the entire assembly over, and check the fabric position from the right side. Adjust as needed, making sure designs are centered properly and that the fabric is straight in both directions.

STEP 4

5 Turn the assembly facedown once again. To attach the fabric to the board, start at the middle of each edge. Draw the fabric onto the back of the board, and staple it in place. Do the same for the opposite edge, pulling the fabric taut and stapling it down. Then do the other two edges. Continue stapling the fabric every inch or so, working from the middle out to the

edges and alternating the sides. When you reach a curved edge, clip the fabric to within 1 inch of the board edge before stapling it down. When you reach the corners, clip out the excess to reduce bulk and staple securely.

STEP 5

6 For a professional finish, line the back of the headboard. Use the piece cut in step 1. Lay the headboard padded side down, and place the lining on top, right side up. Fold in and staple down the edges all around. Glue gimp around the entire edge to hide the staples.

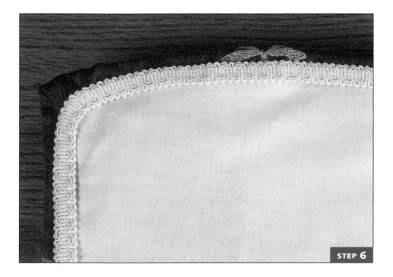

STEP 6

HOMASOTE FIBERBOARD

Homasote fiberboard comes in 4-foot by 8-foot sheets. Turned on its side, it can make a headboard up to 4 feet high for any bed, twin size through king. It can even make a padded backrest for a daybed. If you want to make a headboard that is taller than 4 feet, you will need to use two sheets of Homasote fiberboard. For easier handling, mark and cut out the headboard pieces first, and then join them together on both sides with thin metal mending plates. The plates will not be visible once the headboard is padded and covered with fabric.

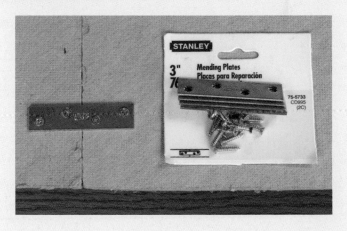

Faux-Fur Throw

A fur throw to drape over a sofa or across the foot of a bed makes a wonderful gift. If you want to make a big hit with a college student, this is the item to make. Since the wrong side of faux fur is nothing to crow about, you'll need to add a lining. My favorite is cotton velveteen; it is soft to the touch, easy to sew on, and wide enough not to require seams. Other options are stretch velour and wool jersey. To make this throw, the fur and the lining are placed back to back and cut out as a large rectangle. The edges are bound with four fabric strips, resulting in perfectly mitered corners. Choose a woven fabric that will hold a crease for the binding. If you are a beginning sewer, choose a printed fabric for the border to hide any imperfections in the mitering.

Solids, prints, and textured fabrics are all appropriate for the mitered binding.

Before You Begin see **Fabric Preparation** on p. 94.

FOR ONE THROW, YOU'LL NEED:

- 2 yards 62- to 64-inch-wide faux fur
- 2 yards 58- to 60-inch-wide cotton velveteen fabric for lining
- 2⅛ yards satin, brocade, or cotton velveteen fabric for binding
- Measuring and marking tools
- General sewing/craft supplies

PREPARING THE FUR

1 Preshrink the fur, backing, and border fabrics in a warm-water wash and permanent-press dryer cycle. Preshinking is especially important when combining fabrics, since all fabrics shrink differently. Omit this step if the finished throw will be dry-cleaned.

[**WORKROOM TIP**] The faux furs available today look and feel incredibly like the real thing. If you have difficulty finding a good selection in your area, check out Carol's Zoo.

2 Choose a work area that can be easily cleaned up; working with faux fur is messy and produces a lot of lint and hairs. Use a large T-square to true up the cut ends of the fur so that they form right angles with the selvages. Straighten the ends of the backing fabric by pulling a crosswise thread or using a T-square and cutting straight across.

3 Lay the fur facedown on a large flat work surface. Lay the backing fabric on the fur, wrong sides together, lining up one selvage and one cut edge. If the backing fabric has a nap, make it run in the same direction as the fur nap. Trim off the excess fur even with the other two edges of the backing fabric. Hand-baste both layers together all around, using very long stitches.

STEP 3

DESIGN IDEA For a lighter-weight throw, cut the body from cashmere or polyfleece. Neither of these fabrics needs to be backed with a lining.

BINDING THE EDGES

1 Cut four strips on the lengthwise grain from the binding fabric. Make each strip 7 inches wide and 2 inches longer than the throw edge. On each strip, press the long edges ½ inch to the wrong side. Then fold each strip lengthwise, wrong side in, letting one side extend ⅛ inch beyond the other to ensure it will catch when the other edge is topstitched. Press to set the crease. Be careful not to stretch the binding.

STEP 1

2 Open out the folds. Place two strips right sides together, with edges and folds matching, so that the wider and narrower sections align with each other. Stitch the short edges together at one end with a ½-inch seam allowance. Measure from the stitching line along each side fold for 3 inches, or the width of the finished binding, and mark a dot. Also mark a dot on the stitching line at the center foldline.

STEP 2

3 Use a ruler and an air-soluble marker to connect the three dots as shown. Machine-stitch on the marked lines, pivoting at the top center dot.

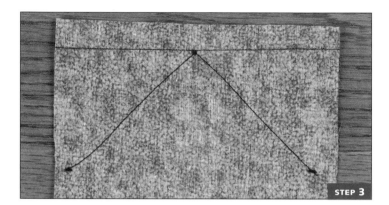

STEP 3

4 Turn the binding right side out. Slip the mitered corner onto a corner of the comforter, and check the size. The narrower edge should go on the fur side and the slightly wider edge on the backing side.

STEP 4

5 Turn the miter inside out again, and trim out the bulk.

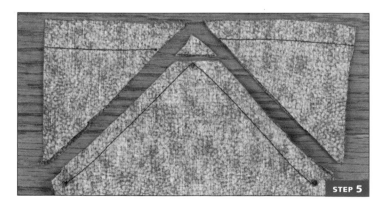

STEP 5

6 Turn the miter right side out, using a point turner to get a sharp point. Slide the blanket into the corner of the binding as far as it will go yet still lie smooth. Pin the corners and edges of the binding to the throw through all layers. When you reach the next corner, trim the strip ½ inch beyond the edge of the throw.

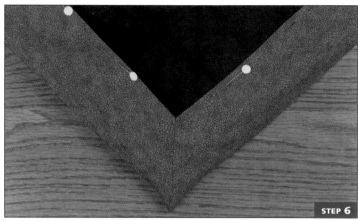

STEP 6

7 Repeat steps 1–6 to join the next strip and miter the corner. Be sure to match up the strips so the narrower width is on the fur side. Continue all around until all four corners are mitered and the binding is pinned all around.

8 Check all your pins to make sure that they capture both edges of the folded-over trim. Set the machine for a 3.5mm stitch length, and attach a walking foot or a Teflon foot. Topstitch along the inner edge of the binding through all layers, pivoting at the corners. To prevent puckering, grab the fabric behind and in front of the needle, and pull it taut with equal pressure from both ends as you sew.

9 Press the binding, using a press cloth, to give it a crisp, flat appearance. Keep the iron off of the faux fur.

[WORKROOM TIP] Silk organza makes a great press cloth. It can withstand high heat, and you can see through it.

Futon Cover

A futon is versatile: It can be a low seat with a backrest, or it can fold out to form a bed for sleeping. In this style, called *shikibuton,* three identical cushions are hinged together in a "Z," enabling the entire futon to fold neatly for storage. Making a cover with three separate cushion compartments can be challenging. Be sure to label your fabric pieces as soon as you cut them to avoid confusion during the assembly.

An all-over pattern, such as the Japanese-inspired fabric used here, is more suitable for a futon cover than a design that needs matching.

Before You Begin see **Making a Zippered Boxing Strip** on p. 49.

FOR A TWIN-SIZE FUTON COVER, YOU'LL NEED:

- Futon
- 4¾ yards 54- to 60-inch-wide fabric
- Three 60-inch zippers
- Measuring and marking tools
- General sewing/craft supplies

MEASURING AND CUTTING THE PIECES

1 Use the worksheet on p. 83 to measure your futon and work out the dimensions for each fabric piece you will need. If your futon cushions are a different size than those shown, adjust the yardage amounts accordingly. The zipper length should be about 5 inches shorter than the zippered boxing strip.

2 Use your measurements to cut one top panel (X), one seat panel (Y), one back panel (Z), three plain boxing strips, and three zippered boxing strips from fabric. Refer to the fabric layout for a twin-size futon if appropriate. Label each piece on the wrong side with tape.

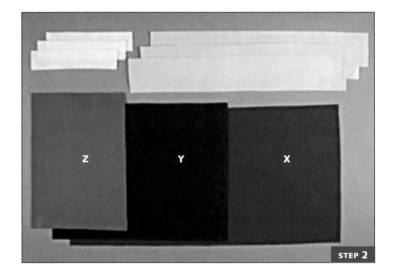

STEP 2

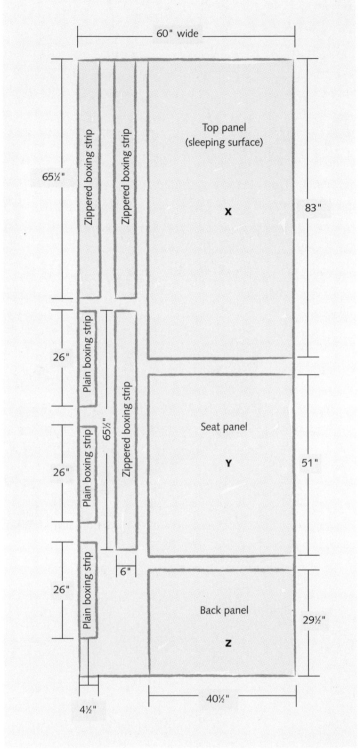

MAKING THE FUTON COVER

1 Cut each zippered boxing strip in half lengthwise. Place each pair right sides together, matching the cut edges. Machine-stitch ¾ inch from the cut edges, using a medium-length stitch for about 3 inches at each end and a long basting stitch in between. Press the seam open, insert the zipper, and remove the basting. Sew each zippered boxing strip to a plain boxing strip with a ½-inch seam allowance.

2 Lay the top panel X right side up on a flat work surface, with the shorter edges at the sides. Measure from the top right corner along the top edge a distance of C, and mark with a pin. Place a zippered boxing strip facedown on the fabric, perpendicular to the long edge and with the right edge aligned on the pin. Machine-stitch ½ inch from the top edge, leaving ½ inch free at each end. The length of the stitching line should equal D.

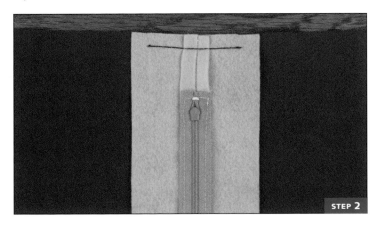

3 Pivot the strip at the top right corner, and pin the long edge to the fabric, right sides together. Pin the entire strip, going around three sides of the large fabric piece, to frame the first seat cushion. Make sure the ends of the boxing strip are directly opposite one another; adjust as needed. Starting where the previous stitching left off, machine-stitch the pieces together with a ½-inch seam allowance. Stop ½ inch from the corner with your needle in the down position. Clip into the boxing-strip seam allowance for ⅜ inch to facilitate pivoting. Lift the presser foot, and turn the work. Continue around, stopping ½ inch from the end of the strip. Pivot the work to sew the short end of the strip to the top panel, to match the other side.

4 To finish framing out this end of the cover, pin the seat panel Y to the boxing strip, right sides together. Make sure the corners align. Machine-stitch around three sides, starting and stopping ½ inch from the end of the boxing strip. The cover for the first cushion is now complete. The fourth "wall" of the boxing strip is the top panel itself. Both panels will have excess fabric hanging loose.

5 To start the second cushion section, pin a new zippered boxing strip to the top panel X immediately adjacent to the first boxing strip. You will be stitching across, as in step 3, leaving ½ inch free at each end. The goal is for the stitching lines on both boxing strips to almost touch. Repin as needed, and then stitch as described.

6 Remove the work from the machine. Pin the boxing strip to the free edges of the seat panel Y, going around three sides, as in step 4. Stitch the pieces together. Stitch the remaining short end of the boxing strip to the top panel X. There should be a free edge of the boxing strip remaining across the middle.

7 Pin the third boxing strip to the side edges of the top panel X and the free edge of the boxing strip from the middle cushion. Stitch the pieces together, using ½-inch seams and stopping ½ inch from the ends of the boxing strip.

8 Pin the back panel Z to the free edges of the boxing strip. Pin the remaining edge to the top panel Y and to the ends of the boxing strip, boxing in the corners. Machine-stitch together. Turn the cover right side out.

9 Open the zippers all the way. Test-fit the foam cushions inside the futon cover, using plastic dry-cleaning bags for easier insertion. Mark stitching lines between the cushions to secure the fabric layers together. Remove the cushions. Lay the cover flat, and stitch as marked. Reinsert each cushion into its own pocket, and zip closed.

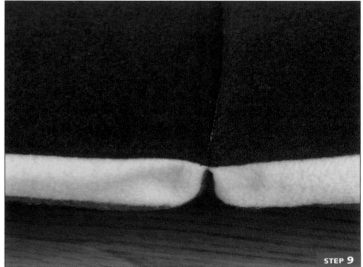

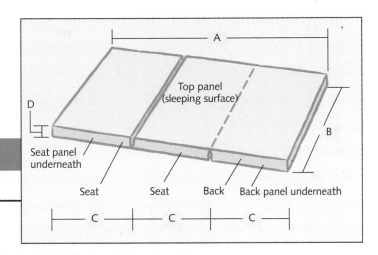

FUTON COVER WORKSHEET

Fill in all the blanks in inches.

FIRST, LAY THE FUTON OUT FLAT AND MEASURE IT.
DIMENSIONS FOR A STANDARD-SIZE FUTON ARE INCLUDED.

		Your Futon	**Standard Twin-Size Futon**
Overall length from end to end	(A)		75"
Width from side to side	(B)		39½"
Length of each cushion	(C)		25"
Depth of each cushion	(D)		3½"

Then determine the size of each fabric piece you will need.

TOP PANEL OR SLEEPING SURFACE (CUT ONE)

Length: A + D + D + 1" _____ 83"

Width: B + 1" _____ 40½"

Seat panel (cut one)

Length: C + C + 1" _____ 51"

Width: B + 1" _____ 40½"

BACK PANEL (CUT ONE)

Length: C + D + 1" _____ 29½"

Width: B + 1" _____ 40½"

PLAIN BOXING STRIP (CUT THREE)

Length: C + 1" _____ 26"

Width: D + 1" _____ 4½"

ZIPPERED BOXING STRIP (CUT THREE)

Length: B + C + 1" _____ 65½"

Width: D + 2½" _____ 6"

Fabric-Covered Walls

There's nothing like fabric-covered walls to make a room cozy, warm, and quiet—and nothing quite as expensive to hire out. Don't let this project intimidate you. It's something you can tackle yourself. To do a complete room, you'll need a large amount of fabric, about two days of time, and one or two friends willing to help you for some of the steps. If a whole room seems too ambitious, start with a single wall, maybe the one behind your bed. Suggested coverings include quilted or textured fabrics, intricate patterns or prints, faille, chintz, and velveteen. Avoid fragile fabrics, such as velvet, that the staples can snag or tear; also avoid stripes and plaids because many walls are not straight.

Before You Begin 🧵 see **Double Welt** on p. 89.

FOR THIS PROJECT, YOU'LL NEED:

- Fabric
- Medium-weight 1-inch-thick batting sold by the yard
- Double-welt cord
- 2 staple guns, hand- or electric-powered (one for each partner)
- 2 boxes of ½-inch staples, one for each gun (1,000 staples per box)
- Elmer's® glue
- One 60-yard roll of Millennium double-sided tape and/or hot-glue gun
- Two 8-foot ladders
- Carpenter's level
- Hammer
- Needle-nose pliers or screwdriver
- Knee pads
- Measuring and marking tools
- General sewing/craft supplies

PLANNING THE PROJECT

1 Use the worksheet on p. 86 to measure your walls and figure out the fabric yardage needed. For a 14-foot by 20-foot room with 10-foot-high ceilings, three large windows, two entry doors, one closet door, and one fireplace, we needed 33 yards of solid-color 54-inch-wide fabric plus 7 yards of fabric to cover 30 yards of double-welt cord on the bias.

2 Use the same worksheet to calculate the batting yardage. Enter the batting width for B, and omit section 4.

3 Purchase your fabric and batting in the required amounts. Also purchase the double-welt cord. To figure out exactly how much cord you need, measure around all the doors, windows, and fireplaces and along all the baseboard, ceiling, and corner joins.

APPLYING THE BATTING

1 Remove all the switch plates and electrical outlet plates. Cut the batting yardage into panels ½ inch shorter than the wall height (1 inch shorter if the ceilings are high) since it will stretch a bit in the application. Working with a partner, start at an inside corner of the wall. Position the cut edge ¼ inch below the top of the wall, and let the long edge fall into the corner. Staple into the batting at the top corner and across the top edge at 16-inch intervals. Hold the staple gun flush with the wall so that the staples go straight into the wall and do not stick out. Leave the side edge loose.

2 At the bottom edge, gently stretch the batting down until it is ¼ inch from the floor or baseboard molding. Staple in place across the bottom edge. Pull some of the batting fibers over the indentation caused by each staple.

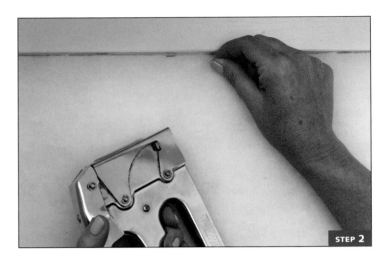

3 Place the second batting panel alongside the first, butting (not overlapping) the long side edges. Staple in place across the top and bottom edges. Continue in this way. When you reach a corner that juts into the room, wrap the batting loosely so that the batting doesn't stretch and pull apart at the corner when the fabric is pulled taut over it.

4 To fit batting around windows and doors, staple next to the opening and then cut away the excess. Carefully cut away the batting around light fixtures and switch plates. When the hardware is reattached later, it will cover up the raw edges. If there are any electrical wires running around the perimeter of the room that you would like to cover, make sure that the wires are in good shape and not frayed. While you may be tempted to tuck these wires behind the batting, it can be a fire hazard so we caution you not to do so.

APPLYING THE FABRIC

1 For your first surface, choose a plain wall without doors or windows. Several fabric panels will be seamed together and stretched across from one corner edge to another. Measure this distance, divide by B on your worksheet, and round up to the nearest whole number to determine how many panels you should sew together. The excess will be trimmed off after the panels are sewed together.

FABRIC-COVERED WALLS WORKSHEET

1. Gather your information.

Fill in the blanks in inches.

Width of each wall to be covered. Measure straight across horizontally, ignoring doors and windows.

_____

Height of wall. Measure from floor to ceiling, or wainscoting to ceiling.

_____

Fabric width, from selvage to selvage

_____

Pattern repeat, if any

_____

2. Determine the number of fabric widths required.

Add the wall widths together. (A)_____.

Enter the fabric width. _____

Subtract 2" for selvage removal and seam allowance. – 2"

The result is the panel width after seaming. (B)_____

Divide A by B. _____

Round up to the nearest whole number. This is the number of fabric widths required. (C)_____

3. Determine the cut panel length.

Enter the wall height. _____

Enter the pattern repeat. _____

Add in a 6" cutting allowance. + 6"

Add these three figures together. This is the cut panel length. (D)_____

4. Determine the double-welt fabric yardage.

A typical room requires 60 yards to 80 yards of welt, depending on the ceiling height. One yard of fabric will make 15 yards of double welt, cut on grain. For a general estimate, allow 1 yard of fabric for each wall, 1⅓ yards for a room with a high ceiling. To figure out exactly how much cord you will need, measure around all the doors, windows, and fireplaces and along all the baseboard, ceiling, and corner joins. Convert your total to yards and divide by 15 to determine the fabric yardage. Jot down your estimate below.

_____ yards of fabric

5. Determine the total fabric yardage.

Multiply C times D. _____

To convert to yards, divide by 36". ÷ 36"

Enter the result. _____ yards of fabric

Enter the yardage estimate from step 4. _____ yards of fabric

Add the last two figures together. This is the total fabric yardage required. _____ yards of fabric

2 Clear a big sewing surface, so that your fabric can fall off the table onto the floor instead of backing up into a wall. Cut several fabric panels to the measurement D in your worksheet, or 6 inches longer than the wall height for a solid fabric, until you have the required number. If the fabric has a pattern repeat, cut the second panel to line up with the pattern of the first, plus an extra 6 inches at the bottom. Cut each new panel in turn the same way. The extra 6 inches will give you an edge to grab onto so that you can pull the fabric taut. Cut off all the selvages so marks or symbols printed on the edge do not show through.

[WORKROOM TIP] Mark the top of each panel with tape as you cut it. That way, you won't accidentally sew one upside down.

3 Place two panels right sides together, and pin the long edges, starting at the top and bottom and easing in the middle. Adjust the pinning and seam allowance as needed to match any patterns. Machine-stitch from top to bottom, using a standard stitch length. Trim the seam allowance to ½ inch, if it is wider from pattern matching. Press the seam open. Repeat to join all the panels for the first wall section. Trim off any excess so the width matches the wall measurement you made in step 1. Press seams open.

4 Start at the top of the wall, where the corner meets the ceiling or molding. It is very important that the first piece is applied square. Line up the top edge of the fabric on the wall, and staple in place. Do not fold or turn under the raw edges—they will be covered with double welt later. Continue stapling every 3 inches. Keep the fabric taut between staples, but do not stretch it. Strive for a consistent tension so that the fabric is not slack or baggy and the pattern is not distorted.

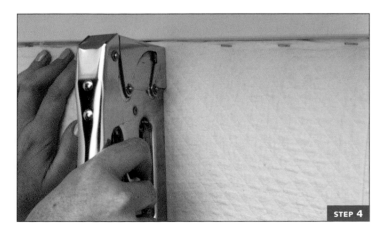

STEP 4

5 Work with a partner, one person stapling and the other a few feet ahead holding the fabric. This enables the person who is stapling to work efficiently. If you must work alone, staple the fabric to the top of the wall a few feet ahead of where you are working to hold it there temporarily and take the drag off the fabric you are handling.

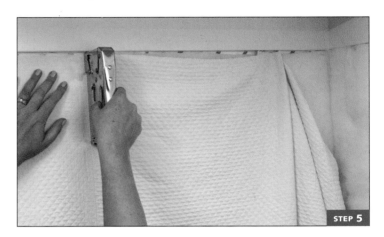

STEP 5

6 After you staple one foot beyond the first seam, stop and check the seam alignment. Pull the seam taut and hold a carpenter's level against it vertically to make sure it is hanging straight. Staple the bottom edge of the seam to the wall about ⅛ inch from the floor or baseboard molding to hold the seam in alignment.

STEP 6

7 Continue stapling along the top edge until you reach one foot beyond the next seam. Repeat step 6. Continue in this way, making certain every seam is perpendicular to the floor and anchoring it at the bottom, until you reach the corner. Any staples that do not go in all the way can be hammered flat for a smooth surface.

8 Return to the corner where you first started. Pull the fabric taut and down to smooth out the wrinkles but not so taut that the seams begin to twist. Staple in place from the top down. Staple the opposite edge into the corner in the same way.

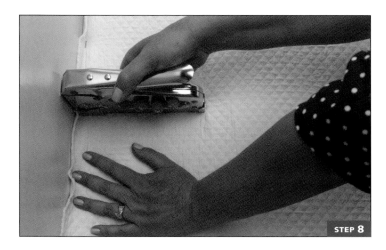

STEP 8

9 Grab onto the 6-inch allowance at the lower edge, pull the fabric taut, and staple the bottom edge to the wall. Place the staples every 2 inches, or closer if needed, so that bulges do not form in between. You may need to remove some staples, adjust the fullness, and then restaple. Make sure you have a smooth surface up and down and into the corners. Once you have a smooth surface in all directions, trim off the excess fabric below the staple line with small sharp scissors.

10 To go around an opening such as a door frame, staple the fabric to the wall above the opening, just below the ceiling, as usual. Cut into the fabric, perpendicular to the ceiling, in the middle of the opening, stopping 4 inches from the top of the opening. Cut diagonally into the corners. Begin stapling close to the edges of the opening all around. If the opening is large, cut away some of the excess fabric in the interior to cut down the drag. Finish by trimming the fabric just beyond the staple line.

STEP 10

APPLYING THE DOUBLE WELT

1 Use the double cord and remaining fabric to make double welt. Cut the fabric strips on grain or on the bias.

2 Use the welt to cover all the raw fabric edges around door and window openings, at wall joins and corners, and along baseboards and ceiling or molding edges. Glue in place or attach with ½-inch-wide double-sided Millennium tape.

[WORKROOM TIP] Another option for covering raw edges is gimp, which retails for about $1 a yard. You can save time by using gimp, but double-welt cord is what professionals use.

TIP

[WORKROOM TIP] You may encounter sections on your wall that are too narrow and awkward to reach with a staple gun but too wide to fill with double welt. An example is a sliver of wall between the moldings of two closely spaced windows (see the photo above). To cover these areas, glue the batting and fabric in place.

DOUBLE WELT

Double welt differs from single welt (see p. 13) in that it has two cords in the casing instead of one. A stitching line between the two cords secures the fabric covering so that no raw edges show. Double welt is used on fabric-covered walls, where it conceals the raw fabric edge along the molding or in the corners, and on furniture, where the raw fabric edge meets the wood. It can be used in place of gimp or flat braid and is a great option when you can't find the right color trim to hide raw edges from view. Here's how to cover the double cord:

1 Cut 2-inch-wide strips of fabric on grain. Piece the strips together diagonally to make one continuous strip long enough for your project. Place the double-welt cord ½ inch from the edge of the fabric.

2 Fold the closer edge over the double cord, covering the full width but no farther.

3 Fold over the entire piece, wrapping the cord completely, for a very tight fit.

4 Without pinning, sew between the two cords using matching thread. Sew slowly, concentrating on the 6 inches immediately in front of the needle and checking the cord to make sure it remains completely covered and snug in the fabric.

5 When you are through sewing, trim off the excess fabric close to the stitching line. Apply the cord to your project with the trimmed edge on the underside.

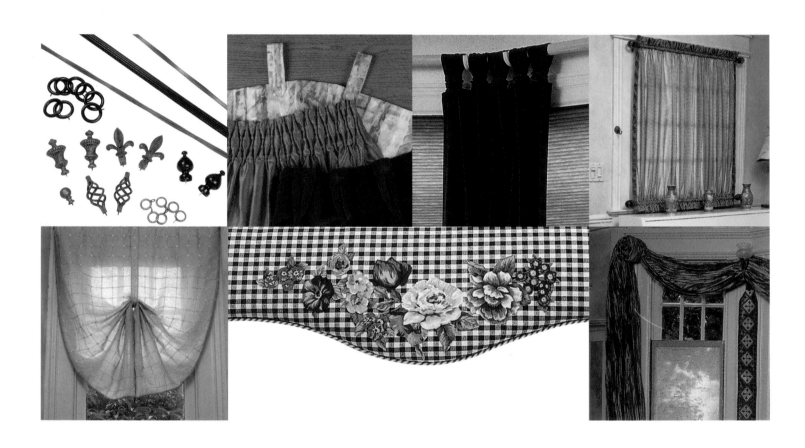

Part 4

WINDOW COVERINGS

Window coverings pull a room together. They can be used in many ways—to dress up a plain window, to carry out a color scheme, or to provide privacy. A window covering can frame an outside view or block an unwanted view. Draperies that draw closed can prevent your furniture and carpets from fading and help cut down on your heating bill. While it generally takes a lot of fabric to cover a window, the sewing skills used to make window treatments are really quite minimal. Header tapes are available that let you create shirring and pleating instantly. Curtain rods and finials act as window jewelry—fun if you are an accessory lover.

Measuring for Window Treatments

The success or failure of a window treatment is determined by the time you spend measuring your windows, so don't rush this process, doing it on the fly as you head out the door to buy the fabric. The most accurate way to measure a window is to use an extra long 120-inch measuring tape and to ask a friend to help. Draw a sketch of the window, measure and jot down the dimensions on the sketch, and then fill in the Drapery Yardage Worksheet. A blank copy of the worksheet, ready to photocopy, is printed on p. 96. Let's take a look at a completed worksheet, one section at a time, so that you can see how the calculations are made. You'll find a calculator helpful.

1. Gather your information. Fill in all the blanks in inches.

Rod length	60"
Overlap and returns allowance	12"
Fabric fullness (circle one)	1½ ② 2½ 3
Fabric width (circle one)	36" 44" ⑤4" 60" 118"
Finished length	84"
Header allowance	8"
Hem allowance	8"
Pattern repeat	27"

GATHERING YOUR INFORMATION

Your first step is to jot down the various measurements you will need. The first section of the worksheet is filled in on the facing page. Let's take a look at each of these measurements one by one.

Rod Length. First, you must decide what type of rod you want to use. Refer to Drapery Rods (p. 102), and visit a well-stocked home-dec store to make your selection. The rod should be 6 inches longer than the window so that it extends 3 inches beyond the window on each side. The rod in our sample worksheet is 60 inches long. You may wish to install the rod at this point.

Overlaps and Returns. Draperies on traverse rods require extra fabric so that the panels can overlap at the center. For a 3-inch center overlap, allow an extra 6 inches. Extra fabric at each end allows the fabric to "return" to the wall and conceal the protruding hardware. Decorative rods with finials and brackets don't usually have overlaps or a return, but you can simulate a return by allowing extra fabric and tacking the curtain to the wall. We've allowed 12 inches in our example for the overlaps and returns.

Fabric Fullness. The fabric fullness is 1½ times to 3 times the rod length, depending on the style of window treatment and the fabric. For example, tab-top draperies require a fullness that is 1½ times the length of the rod. The fullness in our example is 2 times the rod length.

Fabric Width. This measurement is the width of the fabric you will be using. Our sample fabric is 54 inches wide.

Finished Length. The finished length is measured from the top of the header to the bottom edge of the window treatment. Typical finished lengths are ½ inch above the floor, 4 inches below the windowsill, or ½ inch above the sill. When finished, our full-length draperies will measure 84 inches.

Header Allowance. The top of any drapery treatment is referred to as a "header." There are many different header styles, with varying fabric requirements. A pinch-pleat drapery needs a 6-inch to 8-inch header allowance, depending on the size of the crinoline, which can be 3 inches to 4 inches deep. A café-rod treatment without a top ruffle needs a 2-inch header for a 1½-inch rod pocket and a ½-inch seam finish. A café-rod treatment with a top ruffle needs a 6-inch header, which includes a 1½-inch rod pocket, a 2-inch ruffle, and a ½-inch seam finish. If you haven't decided on a header style, simply add 8 inches to have enough for just about any style. An exception is tab tops, which require about ½ yard extra for each drapery width. We allowed 8 inches in our example.

Hem Allowance. The hem is usually 4 inches deep and double turned, making the required allowance 8 inches. That's what we put in our example.

Pattern Repeat. The pattern repeat is measured in inches along the lengthwise grain of the fabric, starting at any point on a pattern and ending at the same spot on the next identical pattern. The pattern repeat on a small check or plaid might be ½ inch, whereas on a large floral print, it might be 27 inches. If your window treatment requires several widths of fabric, you will need to allow for the pattern repeat in each cut length so that the patterns can be matched when the lengths are seamed together. Similarly, if you are making draperies or valances for several windows in a room, you'll want to cut the panels so that the pattern will fall at a consistent height around the room. If you are using a single width of fabric on a small window, you may still want to take the pattern repeat into account, perhaps to center a motif in the middle of the drapery panel.

Center a large motif when the window treatment is one panel wide.

of the TRADE

FABRIC PREPARATION

Follow the steps in the order listed below to perfectly prepare drapery and lining fabrics for cutting and sewing. The same techniques can be used for making duvet covers, pillows, cushion covers, blankets, tablecloths, napkins, and other items where the fabric must be cut on grain.

1 Preshrink the fabric if you are planning to launder the finished item later. If the item will be dry-cleaned, you can skip preshrinking.

2 Cut off the selvages an inch or so in from the edge so that the fabric lies perfectly flat. If left intact, selvages that are stretched and wavy or tightly woven and puckered can distort the fabric and cause it to draw up as it is pressed, dry-cleaned, or laundered.

Wait to trim the selvages if you need to match a pattern repeat or a plaid. Some home-dec fabrics have a small arrow printed on the selvage to indicate the direction of the print or plaid. The color bars printed on the selvage can help you match the patterns. Once you have made use of these clues, then you can trim off the selvages.

3 Straighten the ends of the fabric, so that the crossgrain cuts are perfectly square with the trimmed side edges. Lay the fabric flat. If you are working with lots of yardage, roll out as much fabric as you can. Cut into the fabric for a few inches, close to and parallel to the cut edge made by the fabric store.

Pick out a crossgrain thread along the cut, and draw it out across the entire fabric width. Keep pulling threads, recutting if necessary, until you can get one thread to go all the way across the fabric. Then cut along the thread path for a perfectly straight edge. Use this same technique to cut fabric panels for window treatments or other projects. Measure out the fabric for your first cut length, cut into the edge, pull out a crosswise thread, and cut along the thread path. Cutting a straight edge in this way ensures that window treatments hang straight, seat cushions do not stretch and bag, and napkins remain perfectly square after the first washing.

If the crosswise thread keeps breaking, or if you are working with faux fur, vinyl, leather, or a knit fabric, use an oversized T-square, available at building supply stores, to mark a straight edge instead. Measure along both edges and then cut straight across, from mark to mark.

4 Identify each piece immediately after cutting. Place a short piece of tape at the top of each fabric panel on the wrong side. Even if the fabric does not have an obvious nap or direction, subtle differences may become visible once the panels are sewn together. Identifying the top of each cut piece with tape eliminates the problem altogether. You can write on the tape if you need to label the pieces.

5 Pin the pieces together for sewing. Home-dec professionals sometimes skip pinning, but this is not advised for the hobbyist. To join panels that are the same length, such as for drapery, start by matching and pinning the top and bottom edges. Then pin in between at 12-inch intervals, easing one length to the other. Finally, fill in with additional pins. This method helps distribute the fabric evenly and prevents stretching and distortion. If the panels are not evenly matched, the window treatment will not hang straight.

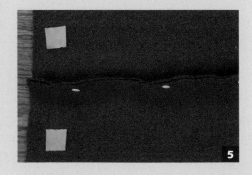

DETERMINING THE FABRIC WIDTHS

The next section of the worksheet is used to calculate the number of fabric widths needed for your window treatment. A simple drapery for a narrow window might take two widths of 54-inch-wide fabric. A larger window might require several 54-inch-wide panels to be seamed together.

---

2. Determine how many fabric widths are required.

Enter the first four figures from section 1 in the appropriate boxes, and do the calculations.

Enter the rod length.	60"
Enter the overlap and returns allowance.	+ 12"
Add these two lengths.	= 72"
Multiply by the fabric fullness.	x 2
The result is the Total Drapery Width (TDW).	= 144"
Divide by the fabric width.	÷ 54"
Enter the result.	= 2.66

Round up to the nearest whole number (round down if the fraction is ¼ or less). This is the number of fabric widths required.   3

As you can see, the calculations are fairly easy to do. The reason the number is rounded up at the end is that it is easier to deal with whole fabric widths. The extra fullness can easily be absorbed in the pleats or drapery folds.

DETERMINING THE CUT LENGTHS

This section is used to determine the cut length of each drapery panel. Here's where we take into account the extra fabric needed for the header, the hem, and any pattern repeats. If you are working with a solid, the first subtotal is the cut length for your fabric. If you are working with a print, enter the pattern repeat and complete the worksheet to obtain the cut length.

---

3. Determine the drapery cut length.

Enter the last four figures from section 1 in the appropriate boxes, and do the calculations.

Enter the desired finished length.	84"
Enter the header allowance.	+ 8"
Enter the hem allowance.	+ 8"
Add these three lengths, and enter the result.	= 100"

This result is the cut length for fabrics without a pattern repeat. Go to section 4 if your fabric does not have a pattern repeat. Continue with this section if your fabric has a pattern repeat.

Divide the cut length by the pattern repeat.	÷ 27"
Enter the result.	= 3.7"
Round up to the nearest whole number.	4
Multiply by the pattern repeat.	x 27"
Enter the result. This is the cut length for fabrics that have a pattern repeat.	= 108"

DETERMINE THE FINAL YARDAGE

The final step is to determine the actual fabric yardage you will need to buy. Enter your final numbers from sections 2 and 3 and perform the calculations.

---

4. Determine the yardage.

Enter your final number from section 2.	3
Enter your final number from section 3.	x 108"
Multiply these two numbers together.	= 324"
Divide the result by 36".	÷ 36"
Enter the result. This is the final yardage needed.	= 9 yards

[WORKROOM TIP] To calculate how much fabric is needed for a lining, use the cut length for fabrics without a pattern repeat.

DRAPERY YARDAGE WORKSHEET

1. Gather your information. Fill in all the blanks in inches.

Rod length   _____

Overlap and returns allowance   _____

Fabric fullness (circle one)   1½   2   2½   3

Fabric width (circle one)   36"   44"   54"   60"   118"

Finished length   _____

Header allowance   _____

Hem allowance   _____

Pattern repeat   _____

2. Determine how many fabric widths are required.

Enter the first four figures from section 1 in the appropriate boxes, and do the calculations.

Enter the rod length.   _____

Enter the overlap and returns allowance.   +_____

Add these two lengths.   =_____

Multiply by the fabric fullness.   x_____

The result is the Total Drapery Width (TDW).   =_____

Divide by the fabric width.   ÷_____

Enter the result.   =_____

Round up to the nearest whole number
(round down if the fraction is ¼ or less).
This is the number of fabric widths required.   _____

3. Determine the drapery cut length.

Enter the last four figures from section 1 in the appropriate boxes, and do the calculations.

Enter the desired finished length.   _____

Enter the header allowance.   +_____

Enter the hem allowance.   +_____

Add these three lengths, and enter the result.   =_____

This result is the cut length for fabrics without a pattern repeat. Go to section 4 if your fabric does not have a pattern repeat. Continue with this section if your fabric has a pattern repeat.

Divide the cut length by the pattern repeat.   ÷_____

Enter the result.   =_____

Round up to the nearest whole number.

Multiply by the pattern repeat.   x_____

Enter the result. This is the cut length for fabrics that have a pattern repeat.   =_____

4. Determine the yardage.

Enter your final number from section 2.   _____

Enter your final number from section 3.   x_____

Multiply these two numbers together.   =_____

Divide the result by 36".   ÷ 36"

Enter the result. This is the final yardage needed.   =_____

Swags

A swag is a stationary window treatment, very dressy yet easy to arrange.

Swags are perfect for the person who craves instant gratification and a classy, dramatic window treatment. The fabric can be draped over brackets, a decorative rod, and sconces—or it can be held to the wall with decorative thumbtacks. Swags are loosely structured and free-spirited, which make them ideal for pleated, wrinkled, or surface-treated fabrics that are interesting in and of themselves. Swags should be lined, and in some cases interlined, because they sag and lose their shape over time.

FOR ONE SWAG, YOU'LL NEED:

- Fabric of your choice
- Lining fabric
- Interlining fabric
- Brackets and mounting hardware
- Double-sided carpet tape or Fun-Tak®
- Rope or welt cord
- Masking tape
- Measuring and marking tools
- General sewing/craft supplies

GETTING STARTED

1 Begin by mounting the brackets that will hold up the swag.

2 Use a rope or welt cord to simulate the drape of the swag on the brackets. Start with one end of the rope just touching the floor. Bring it up and loop it around the first bracket. (You needn't worry about the decorative knots at this stage.) Let the rope drape across the window to the desired depth, and then loop it around the next bracket. Continue until you reach the final bracket. Let the rope cascade down to the floor.

STEP 2

3 Mark the end of the rope with tape. Undo the rope, measure it from the starting end to the tape, and jot down the length. Add 18 inches for each end of the swag for puddling and 18 inches for each bracket for knotting, and convert to yards for your final fabric measurement. Purchase swag fabric, lining fabric, and cotton-flannel interlining fabric in this amount. A cotton-flannel interlining will give the swag a more luxurious appearance and prevent the knots and drape from collapsing over time.

[WORKROOM TIP] Don't skimp on your swag fabric estimate. A swag treatment is effective only if a generous amount of fabric is used in one long continuous piece.

SEWING THE SWAG

1 Lay the swag fabric on a flat surface. If the fabric is pleated, do not spread out the pleats; just let them fall naturally. Measure across the fabric width, and cut the lining and interlining fabrics to match. If the swag fabric is unpleated, cut the lining and interlining 2 inches narrower so that they will not be visible when the swag is installed.

2 Place the swag and lining right sides together, lining up the long edges. Place the interlining underneath, against the wrong side of the lining. Machine-stitch down both long edges through all layers, forming a tube.

STEP 2

3 Press the seam allowance toward the lining. Turn the swag right side out. No hemming is necessary on the ends, since the raw edges will be concealed under the puddling. An exception is sheers.

[WORKROOM TIP] Enclose the raw edge of sheer fabrics with Seams Great for hassle-free hemming. This product makes the edge more stable by eliminating stretching and raveling.

ARRANGING THE SWAG

1 Begin by hanging the swag loosely over the first bracket, allowing 18 inches for puddling on the floor. Some fabrics are easier to control if you pleat them in your hand as you work. Don't worry if you have slightly more than 18 inches for puddling since you can always cut off the excess later.

2 Twist the swag around the bracket in a decorative knot.

3 Drape or knot the swag over the remaining brackets, one by one. This window treatment is unstructured and almost impossible to get absolutely symmetrical, so don't fuss; just have fun. A bit of double-sided carpet tape strategically placed can prevent slippery fabrics from wandering.

4 Arrange the puddles at the base, tucking in the raw edges. Professional-looking puddles have three layers bunched onto the floor. Use double-sided carpet tape or Fun-Tak to hold the puddles in place.

5 Stuff tissue paper or bridal tulle into sections that lack body. Another layer of swag fabric might be needed to achieve fullness between brackets.

Drapery Headings

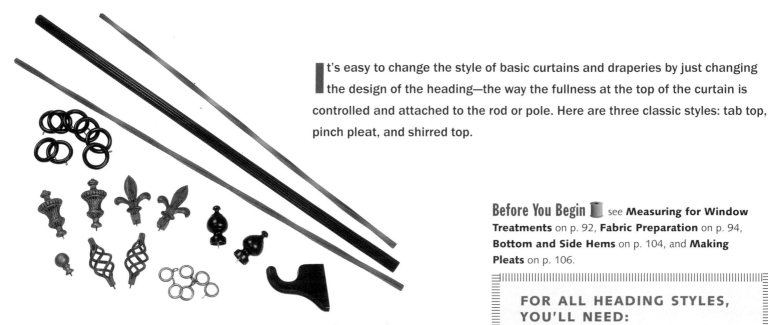

It's easy to change the style of basic curtains and draperies by just changing the design of the heading—the way the fullness at the top of the curtain is controlled and attached to the rod or pole. Here are three classic styles: tab top, pinch pleat, and shirred top.

Decorative drapery rods with their various finials, brackets, and rings heighten our visual pleasure in a window treatment. The rings even make a pleasant sound as the curtains are drawn open and closed.

Before You Begin see **Measuring for Window Treatments** on p. 92, **Fabric Preparation** on p. 94, **Bottom and Side Hems** on p. 104, and **Making Pleats** on p. 106.

FOR ALL HEADING STYLES, YOU'LL NEED:

- Fabric of your choice
- Drapery weights
- Measuring and marking tools
- General sewing/craft supplies

FOR TAB-TOP PANELS, YOU'LL ALSO NEED:

- Drapery rod and hardware
- Buttons (optional)

FOR PINCH-PLEAT DRAPERIES, YOU'LL ALSO NEED:

- Drapery or traverse rod with rings and hardware
- 4-inch-wide crinoline
- Drapery pin hooks

FOR SHIRRED DRAPERIES, YOU'LL ALSO NEED:

- Shirring tape
- Drapery rod with rings and hardware
- Drapery pin hooks

Three different header styles: The pinch-pleat drapery in the foreground can be hung from a traverse rod, as can the shirred panel directly behind it. The tab-top curtain in the background requires a decorative rod.

TAB-TOP DRAPERIES

If you want a tailored look in a room, tab-top draperies may be the answer. They work well in fabrics that take a sharp crease, such as 100 percent linen, decorator-weight cotton, and lightweight canvas. Soft manmade fibers or thick fabrics like chenille may look trendy, but they will not hang in neat folds close to the window. Don't overlook tab tops for valances; just jot down a shorter length on your Drapery Yardage Worksheet to calculate the yardage.

GETTING STARTED

1 Decide how much of a drop you want from the top of the rod to the top of the drapery where the tabs will be joined. You may, for instance, want to see part of the window peeking out at the top. To hide the window from view, you can mount the rod higher or use shorter tabs. Once you have worked out the desired look, mount the rod above the window. Wooden or wrought-iron rods are good choices for tab-top draperies because the rod is so visible.

2 Complete the Drapery Yardage Worksheet. In section 1, use 1½ for the fabric fullness, ½ inch for the header allowance, and 8 inches for the hem allowance. To calculate the tab and facing fabric requirements, multiply the final result in section 2 (the number of fabric widths required) by ½ yard. Add this number to your total in section 4 to obtain the final yardage requirement. Purchase the fabric in this amount.

CUTTING THE PANELS AND FACING

1 Prepare the fabric for sewing.

2 Cut the individual panels according to your Drapery Yardage Worksheet. The final number in section 2 tells how many panels to cut. The final number in section 3 tells how long to make each panel. Also cut one facing, 5 inches deep by the full fabric width for each panel. Use the remaining fabric for the tabs.

MAKING THE TABS

1 Decide on the number of tabs and their spacing. A standard look is five to seven tabs spaced 7 inches to 9 inches apart across a 54-inch-wide drapery panel.

DESIGN IDEA Tabs that are spaced far apart will allow the fabric to swag in between, revealing the facing. You can accentuate the swags by cutting the facing from a contrasting fabric. Buttons on the tabs will attract additional attention to the header.

2 Decide on the tab width and length. A typical finished size is 1¼ inches wide by 11 inches long to fit over a 1⅜-inch-diameter rod. To make tabs this size, cut one 4½-inch by 12-inch strip of fabric for each tab desired. For button-on tabs, cut two 2½-inch by 14-inch strips for each tab desired. Fabric ties are narrower, typically 1 inch wide. For fabric ties, cut one 3-inch by 12-inch strip for each tie. Make your tabs or ties 1¼ inches longer for a 2½-inch-diameter rod.

[WORKROOM TIP] Wrap a cloth tape measure around the rod to help you determine the distance from the top of the drapery around the rod. Make a tab in scrap fabric, and try it on the rod before cutting out all of the tabs from the decorator fabric.

3 To sew plain tabs or ties, fold each strip in half lengthwise, right side in. Sew across the short end and down the long edge with a ½-inch seam allowance. Press the seam allowance back onto the tab or tie to facilitate turning. Trim the seams to ⅛ inch, and clip the corners diagonally. Turn right side out, press well, and pound flat.

STEP 3

4 To sew button tabs, place the fabric strips right sides together in pairs. Cut a 1½-inch by 3-inch rectangle from paper. Trim off two corners diagonally so that the end comes to a point. Place the paper template on the fabric, and trace around the point and adjacent sides.

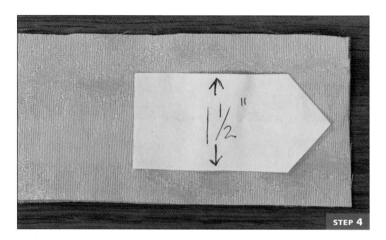
STEP 4

5 Sew along both long edges and around the point in a ½-inch seam allowance. Trim and turn as in step 3.

SCRAPS *of* Knowledge

DRAPERY RODS

Drapery rods can be either decorative or strictly utilitarian. Every rod needs to be supported by a bracket at each end and sometimes in the middle as well, depending on the length and composition of the rod. Supports for wrought-iron rods, for example, must be spaced every 4½ feet to 5 feet to prevent the rod from bending. Wooden rods can span a longer distance, up to 6 feet, between brackets. The style of rod and bracket you choose is as much a part of the window treatment as the fabric panels you design.

Decorative rods can be used for tab-top curtains, curtain headers attached to rings, and stationary window treatments, such as swags. For draperies that open and close, you may prefer a traverse rod. With this rod, the draperies are mounted on a hidden track and can be opened and closed using a draw cord. Since you are not tugging on the panels themselves, they are less likely to stretch out of shape or become soiled with fingerprints.

SEWING THE DRAPERIES

1 Join the drapery panels together along the side edges with a ½-inch seam allowance to make the number of full panels required. You probably have planned for two panels that hang down from the rod and can be drawn aside at the middle. For a single window, you may not have to do any seaming at all—each panel may simply be one fabric width wide. If you are starting off with an odd number of panels, you will need to cut one of them in half lengthwise and use one piece for each side. Plan so that these narrower panels will fall along the outer edges of the window rather than toward the center when the draperies are hung. Join the facings together to correspond to the panels.

2 Fold and press a 4-inch double-fold hem along the bottom edge of each panel. Topstitch or blindstitch in place.

STEP 2

3 Fold and press a 1½-inch double-fold hem along both side edges of each panel. Machine-stitch in place, stopping 3 inches from the bottom edge. Tack a drapery weight—a flat metal weight covered in plastic or Pellon®—to each bottom corner. Hand-sew the final 3 inches.

STEP 3

4 Fold and press one long edge of each facing ½ inch to the wrong side. If the fabric is bulky, serge this edge and do not turn under.

STEP 4

5 Lay each drapery panel flat, right side up. Fold one tab in half, raw edges together, and pin the raw edges of the tab to a top corner of the panel so that all the raw edges are matching. Pin a second tab to the other top corner. Pin the remaining tabs evenly spaced in between, folding the edge of the panel in half and then in quarters to help determine the correct tab location. Measure to double-check all your tab positions, and adjust as needed. If you made button tabs, pin only the raw edge to the drapery panel, as shown. If you made ties, pin two ties at each location in the same way.

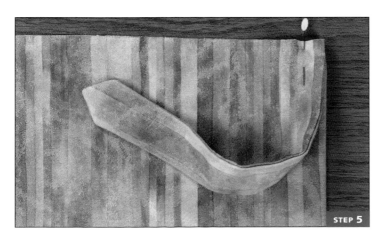

STEP 5

6 Place the facing on the drapery panel, right sides together, matching the long raw edges and letting the facing extend beyond the drapery evenly at each side. Pin in place. Machine-stitch along the top edge with a ½-inch seam allowance, enclosing the tabs or ties in the seam. Grade the seam allowances to cut down on bulk.

STEP 6

7 Fold and press the facing to the wrong side of the drapery panel. Blindstitch or hand-tack the folded edge of the facing to the wrong side of the drapery. Fold in the excess facing fabric at each end, and sew in place. To complete button tabs, fold the pointed end of each tab onto the right side of the panel and sew on a button, tacking through all thicknesses.

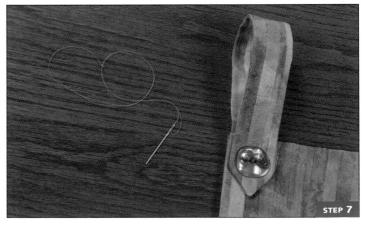

STEP 7

[WORKROOM TIP] When you finish sewing your tab-top draperies, hang them on the rod and arrange the fabric in even folds with the window exposed or as you would like the folds to stack off of the window. Secure at the lower hem with pins or clothespins. Use a steamer to set the folds. Let hang for 24 hours before removing pins.

PINCH-PLEAT DRAPERIES

Pinch pleats make elegant headings for draperies. They are more formal than other headings so use them accordingly. The fullness of pinch pleats is perfect under a valance since the fabric stacks nicely off of the window. Pleat spacing, size, and style are all variables, giving you many ways to customize the panels.

GETTING STARTED

1 Decide what type of rod you would like to use. The finished drapery is hung by drapery pin hooks, which are pinned into the pleats and then hung from rings on the drapery rod. There are decorator rods with rings, which would allow you to easily pull the drapery open and closed by hand, or you might choose a traverse rod with hidden rings and a draw cord. Once you have worked out the desired look and function, mount the rod above the window.

2 Complete the Drapery Yardage Worksheet. In section 1, use 2½ for the fabric fullness, 8 inches for the header allowance, and 8 inches for the hem allowance. Multiply the final number in section 2 (the number of fabric widths required) by the fabric width to determine how many inches of crinoline you'll need. Purchase the fabric, the crinoline, and a lining fabric, if desired.

CUTTING AND SEWING THE PANELS

1 Prepare the fabric for sewing.

2 Cut the individual panels according to your Drapery Yardage Worksheet. The final number in section 2 tells you how many panels to cut. The final number in section 3 tells how long to cut each panel.

[WORKROOM TIP] If you do not have a large table for big projects, move the furniture back to make an open space on the floor. Put pets outside or in another room so that they don't decide to sit in the middle of your work area.

3 Join the cut panels together along the side edges to make up the required width. Window treatments that open in the middle need two panels, which means dividing the available width in half. If you are starting off with an odd number of cut panels, you will need to cut one of them in half length-

TRICK of the TRADE

BOTTOM AND SIDE HEMS

In apparel sewing, hemming is the last step. When you make window treatments, hemming is done early on, right after the fabric widths are sewn together. If the panel is to be lined, cut the lining 3 inches shorter than the decorator fabric, and hem the lining with a 2-inch double-fold hem and the decorator fabric with a 4-inch double-fold hem. Place the lining and the decorator fabric wrong sides together with the lining hem 1 inch higher than the drapery hem. From this point on, treat both layers as one.

Bottom hems are usually double-folded at 4 inches deep, requiring 8 inches of fabric. The weight of this nice, deep hem helps the drapery to hang straight. If the fabric is too bulky for a double-fold hem, allow for a 4-inch single-fold hem instead and serge the raw edge. Machine-stitch or blindstitch in place. (See Blindstitch Foot on p. 108.)

Side hems on drapery panels are usually double-folded at 1½ inches wide. This means you should allow 3 inches extra on each side of a drapery panel for the side hems. Once the side hems are pressed, blindstitch them in place. Velvet draperies should be tacked by hand so that the stitches will not be visible. Another option is to topstitch the side hems with a twin needle so that the stitching becomes a decorative element.

Pillowcasing the lining is another hem option. This method is suitable for lightweight fabrics or very short drapery treatments, such as valances. Cut the drapery and lining fabric to the exact same size. Place the pieces right sides together, and machine-stitch around the side and bottom edges. Turn right side out and press. Fold down the top edge and topstitch to make a casing large enough for the curtain rod.

wise and use one piece for each side. Plan so that these narrower cut panels fall along the outer edges of the window rather than toward the center when the draperies are hung. Press the seams flat.

4 Fold and press a 4-inch double-fold hem along the bottom edge of each panel. If the fabric is bulky, such as the velvet used here, make a 3⅞-inch double-fold hem instead. Topstitch or blindstitch in place.

5 Fold and press a 1½-inch double-fold hem along both side edges of the panel. If the fabric is bulky, make the first fold 1⅛ inches instead of 1½ inches. Machine-stitch in place, stopping 3 inches from the bottom edge. Tack a drapery weight—a flat metal weight covered in plastic or Pellon—to each bottom corner. Hand-sew the final 3 inches.

PLEATING THE HEADER

1 Lay the panel wrong side up on a flat surface. Place the crinoline on top, edges matching. Trim the ends of the crinoline ¼ inch in from the side edges. Fold the header and crinoline down for 4 inches, using the edge of the crinoline as a guide. Fold again, enclosing the crinoline inside. Do not stitch.

2 Measure 3½ inches in from each side to allow for the overlaps and returns, and mark with pins. Work out the pleat size and spacing. Use pins to mark the beginning and end of each pleat across the header.

3 To anchor the pleats, fold the header wrong side in, bringing two pleat pins together. Pin through all the layers. Machine-stitch from the top of the header 4 inches down to the base of the crinoline. Repeat for each pleat across the header.

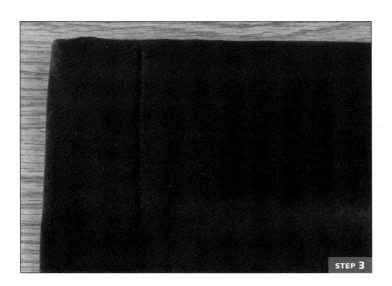

STEP 3

DESIGN IDEA Once the initial pleat is stitched, the fabric can be manipulated any number of ways. For a butterfly pleat, divide it into two even sections instead of three. For a goblet pleat, form three sections, secure with a bar tack, and then stuff batting in the top to puff out the shape. Add a decorative or fabric-covered button over the bar tack as an embellishment. Visit model homes to see more variations on the base pleat.

4 Manipulate the fabric for each pleat into three sections. Make a hand or machine bar tack about 3½ inches from the top through all the layers to hold the pleat in place. Insert drapery pin hooks into the back of each pleat and along the side hems, and hang on the rod.

STEP 4

MAKING PLEATS

Figuring out the number, size, and spacing for pleats on a drapery is not difficult if you take it step by step.

Pleats typically take 4 inches to 6 inches of fabric and are spaced 4 inches to 6 inches apart—about 1 pleat every 10 inches. Use this rule of thumb to decide how many pleats a drapery panel can take. To figure out the pleat size, pinch the header of your drapery panel into a double or triple pleat to see what works for your particular fabric. Then open out the pleat, and measure the fabric that was used. If your pleat took 5 inches of fabric, then five pleats will use 25 inches. The fabric required for all the pleats is called the "pleat allowance." To figure out the spacing between the pleats, measure the distance between the overlap and return pins, subtract the pleat allowance, and divide by 4 (the number of pleats minus 1).

Let's say you started with a 54-inch-wide panel. If the side hems use 3 inches each, the overlap and return allowances use 3½ inches each, and the five pleats use 25 inches, that leaves 16 inches for the four spaces, or 4 inches between each pleat.

[WORKROOM TIP] Pinch-pleat draw-cord tape is a quick way to make pleated draperies. The tape is sewn to the header and works like a shirring tape. The pleats are easy to make, but there is little room for creativity.

SHIRRED-TOP DRAPERIES

Shirring tape provides an elegant topping for sheer or lightweight fabrics. While the effect may look intimidating to sew, making these draperies is actually a snap, thanks to shirring tape. What would we do without these time-savers?

GETTING STARTED

1 Decide what type rod you would like to use. The finished drapery is hung by drapery pin hooks, which are pinned into the shirring tape and then hung from rings on the drapery rod. There are decorative rods with rings, which would allow you to easily pull the drapery open and closed by hand, or you might choose a traverse rod with hidden rings and a draw cord. Keep in mind that the thickness of the shirring tape hinders the stacking at each side of the window when the draperies are drawn back. You may wish to extend the rod past the window to accommodate the extra fabric and maximize the view. Shirred-top draperies can also function as stationary panels. Once you have worked out the desired look and function, mount the rod above the window.

2 Complete the Drapery Yardage Worksheet. In section 1, use 2½ for the fabric fullness (3 if the fabric is sheer), 1 inch for the header allowance, and 8 inches for the hem allowance. Multiply the final number in section 2 (the number of fabric widths required) by the fabric width to determine how much inches of shirring tape you'll need. Purchase the fabric and the shirring tape.

CUTTING AND SEWING THE PANELS

1 Prepare the fabric for sewing.

2 Cut the individual panels according to your Drapery Yardage Worksheet. The final number in section 2 tells how many panels to cut. The final number in section 3 tells how long to make each panel.

3 Join the cut panels together along the side edges to make up the required width. Windows treatments that open in the middle need two panels, which means dividing the available width in half. If you are starting off with an odd number of cut panels, you will need to cut one of them in half lengthwise and use one piece for each side. Plan so that these narrower cut panels fall along the outer edges of the window rather than toward the center when the draperies are hung.

[WORKROOM TIP] When sheer fabric panels are seamed or serged together, the result is a visible join. For a neater appearance, use 118-inch-wide fabric for sheer panels, and avoid the seams altogether.

4 Fold and press a 4-inch double-fold hem along the bottom edge of each panel. Topstitch or blindstitch in place.

STEP 4

5 Fold and press a 1½-inch double-fold hem along both side edges of each panel. Machine-stitch in place, stopping 3 inches from the bottom edge. Tack a drapery weight—a flat metal weight covered in plastic or Pellon—to each bottom corner. Hand-sew the final 3 inches.

STEP 5

SHIRRING THE HEADER

1 Fold and press the top edge of each drapery panel 1 inch to the wrong side. (To avoid excess bulk, do not double-fold here.) Place the shirring tape right side up on the panel, about ¼ inch below the folded edge.

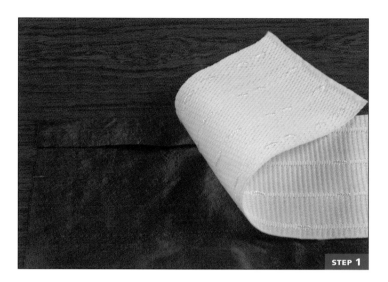

STEP 1

DESIGN IDEA For a decorative ruffled header, use 5 inches as the header allowance on the Worksheet. Fold and press the top edge of the drapery 2½ inches to the wrong side, and install the shirring tape 2 inches below the fold.

2 Fold in the excess tape ¼ inch from each end, leaving the strings exposed and free. Pin the shirring tape in place. Sew one row of machine stitching on each side of every string. Knot the strings at one end of the header.

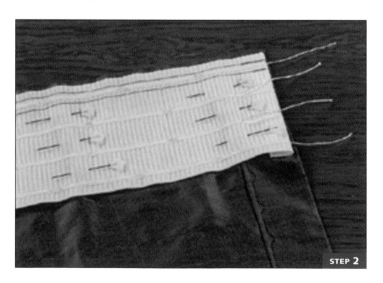

STEP 2

3 To shirr the header, pull all strings at the unknotted end at the same time to the desired fullness. Insert drapery pin hooks into the top of the tape at 5-inch intervals. Hang the hooks from the rod rings.

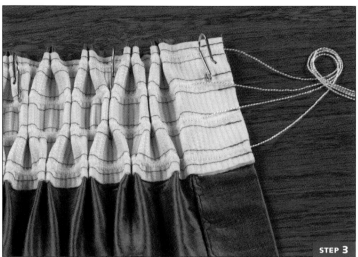

STEP 3

TRICK of the TRADE

BLINDSTITCH FOOT

A blindstitch foot can save you hours of time in home-dec sewing. It is perfect for both the bottom and side hems on window coverings. When coarse-weave fabrics are used, the blindstitches truly are hidden—something that is not always true in apparel sewing.

Most sewing machines can accommodate a blindstitch foot. Every machine is different, but your manual will show you what the foot looks like and what sewing-machine stitch and needle position to use.

The fabric setup is basically the same for all machines. Press both hem folds into position. Fold the pressed hem under and out of view, exposing about ¼ inch of the inner fold allowance. Lay the work on the plate of the sewing machine with the pressed fold at the right. Stitch along this exposed edge. Every few stitches, the needle will jump across and catch the adjacent folded edge. Always practice blindstitching on a scrap of the project fabric to get the stitch length and width at the proper adjustment.

Collared Tab-Top Draperies

This tab-top variation is suitable for plush fabrics, such as the velvet used here, and a hefty decorative drapery rod. A fabric collar encircles the base of each tab, adding a soft, sculptural quality to both the tabs and the folds that are created when the drapery is drawn back from the window.

Before You Begin see **Tab-Top Draperies** on p. 101, **Measuring for Window Treatments** on p. 92, **Fabric Preparation** on p. 94, and **Bottom and Side Hems** on p. 104.

FOR COLLARED TAB-TOP PANELS, YOU'LL NEED:

- Fabric of your choice
- Lining fabric
- 2-inch-diameter drapery rod and hardware
- Drapery weights
- Measuring and marking tools
- General sewing/craft supplies

Collared tab tops look especially lush in cotton velveteen.

GETTING STARTED

1 Choose and mount your drapery rod. The rod shown is 2 inches in diameter. See Getting Started, step 1 on p. 101 for more information.

2 Complete the Drapery Yardage Worksheet. In section 1, use 1½ for the fabric fullness, ½ inch for the header allowance, and 4 inches or 8 inches for the hem allowance, depending on how bulky the fabric is. To calculate the tab and facing fabric requirements, multiply the final result in section 2 (the number of fabric widths required) by ¾ yard. Add this number to your total in section 4 to obtain the final yardage requirement. Purchase the fabric in this amount.

CUTTING THE PANELS AND FACING

1 Prepare the drapery and lining fabrics for sewing.

2 Cut the individual drapery panels according to your Drapery Yardage Worksheet. The final number in section 2 tells how many panels to cut. The final number in section 3 tells how long to make each panel. Also cut one facing, 5 inches deep by the full fabric width for each panel. Use the remaining drapery fabric for the tabs.

3 Cut a lining panel for each drapery panel. Make the lining panels the same width as, but 3 inches shorter than, the drapery panels.

MAKING THE TABS AND COLLARS

1 Decide on the number of tabs and their spacing. The drapery shown uses five tabs across a 50-inch-wide panel. You can use more or fewer tabs, as desired.

2 Decide on the tab width and length, and cut the tabs to this size. The tabs used here were cut 6½ inches wide by 16 inches long. They were tapered by measuring out from each corner 1¾ inches on the short edge and 4 inches on the long edge, and then cutting diagonally from point to point. Adjust the size if your drapery rod is smaller.

3 Cut a collar for each tab 8 inches long and 8¾ inches wide.

4 Press the two longer edges of each tab ⅜ inch to the wrong side. Blindstitch or topstitch in place.

5 Press the two longer edges of each collar ⅜ inch to the wrong side. Blindstitch or topstitch in place. Fold the collar in half, right side in, and stitch the shorter edges together with a ¼-inch seam allowance to make a tube.

SEWING THE DRAPERIES

1 Join the drapery panels together along the side edges with a ½-inch seam allowance to make the number of full panels required. Join the lining panels and the facings in the same way, as required. See Sewing the Draperies, step 1 on p. 102 for more information.

2 Fold and press a 4-inch single- or double-fold hem along the bottom edge of each full drapery panel, depending on the fabric thickness and your earlier calculations. Topstitch or blindstitch in place. Fold and press a 2-inch double-fold hem on each full lining panel. Machine-stitch in place. Place the drapery and lining panels wrong sides together, with the top and side edges matching. The hemmed edge of the lining should fall 1⅝ inches above the hemmed edge of the drapery.

STEP 2

3 Treating the layered fabrics as one, fold and press a 1½-inch double-fold hem on each side edge. Trim off 1 inch of the lining fabric from each edge if necessary to reduce bulk. Machine-stitch in place, stopping 3 inches from the bottom edge. Tack a drapery weight—a flat metal weight covered in plastic or Pellon—to each bottom corner. Hand-sew the final 3 inches (see p. 102, step 3).

STEP 3

4 Lay each drapery panel flat, right side up. Fold one tab in half, wrong side in and raw ends matching. Pin the tab to the top of the panel, 1½ inches in from the top corner. Pin a second tab 1½ inches from the other top corner. Pin the remaining tabs evenly spaced in between, folding the edge of the panel in half and then in quarters to help determine the correct tab location. Measure to double-check all your tab positions, and adjust as needed.

STEP 4

5 Fold and press one long edge of each facing ½ inch to the wrong side. You can also serge this edge, if you prefer, eliminating the fold. Place the facing on the drapery panel, right sides together, matching the long raw edges and letting the facing extend evenly at each side. Pin in place. Machine-stitch along the top edge with a ½-inch seam allowance, enclosing the tabs or ties in the seam. Grade the seam allowances to cut down on bulk.

STEP 5

6 Open out the facing, fold the seam allowances toward the facing on the underside, and edgestitch along the facing edge through all layers.

STEP 6

7 Turn the facing to the wrong side. Fold in the excess facing fabric at each end and sew in place. Bar-tack under each tab through all the layers to hold the facing in place. The bar tacks make a neater appearance than topstitching.

STEP 7

8 To hang the draperies, slip a collar over each tab and then slide the rod through the tab loops.

[**WORKROOM TIP**] Velvet, with its sensitive nap, always poses challenges. Always cut off the selvages; if you don't, the side hems of the drapery panels will draw up and get worse with every dry cleaning. Mark the nap direction on all your cut pieces, including the collars and tabs, so that everything runs in the same direction. A small piece of tape marked with an arrow on the back of every piece is all it takes. Hems are best done by hand. A presser foot smashes the nap, making the hem too visible.

SCRAPS *of* Knowledge

DRAPERY LINING

Adding a lining to a home-dec project is bit like wearing a slip under a dress. The fabric hangs without clinging, it has more body, and there is no translucent show-through. When a window treatment is used to visually enlarge the size of the window, a lining will prevent you from seeing where the window ends and the wall begins. The most compelling reason to line window treatments is to protect decorator fabrics from fading.

Drapery lining comes in ivory and white. Choose whichever one blends in with your shades or shutters, and use the same color throughout the house so that all the windows look the same when viewed from the street.

There are three basic weights to chose from: lightweight, medium-weight, and heavyweight. Lightweight lining fabrics include a cotton/polyester blend called Rain-No-Stain®. In the medium-weight category, there is Special Suede, a 50 percent cotton/50 percent polyester that feels like it has a bit of rubber in it. The most popular heavyweight lining is Black Out, a 50 percent cotton/50 percent polyester lining that actually blacks out all light. Lighter-weight linings work well for draperies made from heavier fabrics, to prevent them from becoming so heavy that they pull the brackets off the wall. Medium-weight fabrics can be used to line pretty much any fabric. Sheers can be backed with another layer of the same sheer fabric.

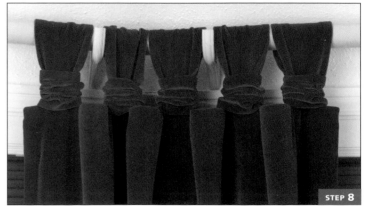
STEP 8

Curtains with Top and Bottom Rods

This window treatment is most commonly used on doors with glass windows and on windows that do not open and close. Its function is to provide privacy while still admitting light, so choose the fabric accordingly. Sheer fabric in a light color will admit the most light.

Before You Begin 🧵 see **Measuring for Window Treatments** on p. 92, **Fabric Preparation** on p. 94, and **Bottom and Side Hems** on p. 104.

FOR ONE CURTAIN PANEL, YOU'LL NEED:

- Two spring-tension or café rods
- Fabric for curtain panel
- Contrasting fabric for headers
- Decorative ribbon at least ⅜ inch wide
- General sewing/craft supplies

Curtains with top and bottom rods can be sized to fit windows of any length.

GETTING STARTED

1 Decide what type of rod you would like to use. This window treatment uses a set of two rods, one for the top rod pocket of the curtain panel and one for the bottom rod pocket. Spring-tension rods mounted inside the window frame are one possibility, but most typically, the rods are mounted outside the window, 2 inches above and 2 inches below the glass. Café rods or decorative curtain rods are suitable choices. Once you have worked out the desired look and function, mount the two rods at the window or door.

2 To determine the panel size, measure the length of one rod and the distance between the rods. Cut the curtain panel 2 times wider than the rod length (2½ if the fabric is sheer) and 1 inch longer than the distance between rods (for the seam allowances).

3 Complete the Contrasting Header Worksheet. The final result is the amount of fabric needed for one contrasting header. Cut two headers, one for each curtain rod. In the project shown, the headers feature the same stripe design as the curtain panel but in a different color. The stripes run in different directions for added contrast.

4 Add one curtain-panel length (from step 2) and two header lengths (from step 3). Multiply by 2. Purchase decorative ribbon in this amount for the side edges of the curtain.

SEWING THE CURTAINS

1 Sew the headers to the top and bottom edges of the panel, right sides together, with ½-inch seams. Press each seam toward its header.

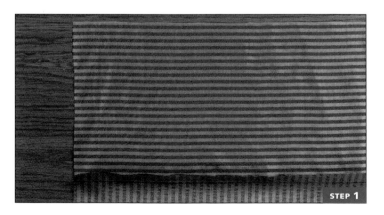

2 Press the long side edges of the entire panel ⅜ inch to the *right* side. Place the decorative ribbon on top, right side up and aligned with the folded edge. Topstitch down both edges of the ribbon, concealing the raw edge.

3 Press the long raw edge of each header ½ inch to the wrong side. To form each rod pocket, fold down again, about ⅛ inch past the seam. Pin in place.

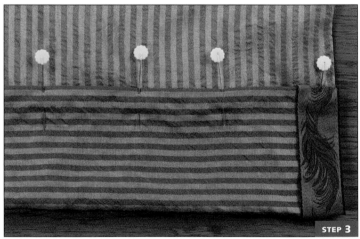

DESIGN IDEA The curtain can also be made from a single sheer fabric, without the contrasting headers and decorative ribbon. Just cut a longer piece for the panel at the start, factoring in the headers minus the additional seam allowances. Make double-fold hems along the side edges.

4 On the right side, stitch in the seam ditch, catching in the pinned edge as you go. Make a parallel row of stitching, measuring in from the outside folded edge, to create the ruffled header and rod pocket. (Consult your worksheet for the sizes.) Press well. Finish by inserting the curtain rods and mounting the panel.

STEP 4

⌐ **WORKROOM TIP** ⌐ The rod pocket size can change with the thickness of the fabric. Make a sample with your intended fabric to avoid ripping out later.

ROD POCKET CHART

Rod Size	Pocket Size
5⁄16" sash rod	5⁄8"
5⁄8" oval rod	1"
7⁄16" sash rod	1"
9⁄16" rod	1"
7⁄8" rod	1½"
13⁄16" rod	1½"
1⅜" wood pole	3"
2½" continental rod	3½"
4½" continental rod	5½"
Round poles	2 times the pole diameter

CONTRASTING HEADER WORKSHEET

Fill in the first three blanks, referring to the descriptions and charts below. Then perform the calculations.

Desired ruffled-header size	_____
Rod pocket size (see chart)	_____
Rod take-up (see chart)	_____
Add ½" seam allowance.	+ ½"
Subtotal	_____
Multiply subtotal by 2.	x 2
Amount needed for each header	_____

DESIRED RUFFLED HEADER SIZE. The ruffled header is the excess fabric beyond the rod pocket. The size is up to you. A typical size is 2 inches long.

ROD POCKET SIZE. The rod pocket size is determined by the diameter of the curtain rod—the larger the rod, the deeper the channel. Refer to the chart below left to find the appropriate pocket size for your rod.

ROD TAKE-UP. The rod take-up accounts for the additional fabric needed to go around the girth of the rod. If you do not allow for take-up, the drapery is shortened as the fabric follows the girth of the rod. Refer to the chart below to find the take-up for your rod.

ROD TAKE-UP CHART

Rod Size	Take-Up Amount
Oval rod	½"
Spring-pressure rod	½"
2½" continental rod	¼"
4½" continental rod	½"
1⅜"-diameter pole	1½"
2"-diameter pole	2"

Cornice Box

A cornice box adds a nice finish to a window treatment as well as a cozy-cottage feel to the room. A cornice box installed close to the ceiling can make the windows look taller. Best of all, you can build and install this box yourself. It's made from Homasote fiberboard, which is lightweight and easy to cut.

Keep the curved edge simple for a box that is graceful as well as easy to build.

Before You Begin see **Single Welt** on p. 13.

FOR ONE CORNICE BOX, YOU'LL NEED:

- Homasote fiberboard (sold in building supply stores)
- Decorator fabric
- Drapery lining fabric
- Self-fabric or contrasting welt
- Gimp
- ½-inch-thick batting
- 1⅝-inch drywall or deck screws
- L-shaped brackets

- Metal mending plates for boxes longer than 8 feet
- Fabric glue
- Spray adhesive or glue gun
- Staple gun with ⅜-inch staples
- Skilsaw® or small pruning saw
- Hand tools
- Measuring and marking tools
- General sewing/craft supplies

CONSTRUCTING THE BOX

1 Determine an appropriate width (W), length (L), and depth (D) for your cornice box, and jot down your figures for W, L, and D. The box must extend beyond the curtain rod under it, cover the tops of the current window treatment, and be deep enough to accommodate any protruding items, such as shutters or twin traverse rods. A typical cornice box extends 3 inches beyond the window on each side and is 4 inches to 8 inches deep.

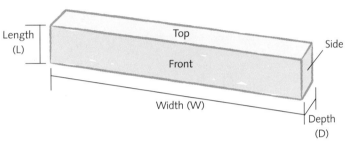

Sketch and jot down the dimensions for your cornice box.

2 Mark and cut the pieces for your box from ½-inch-thick Homasote fiberboard, using your W, L, and D measurements. For the front, cut a piece W by L. For the top, cut a piece W by D minus ½ inch. For the sides, cut two pieces, each D minus ½ inch by L minus ½ inch. Label all four pieces. If your W measurement is longer than 8 feet, you will need to cut two pieces and brace them together with mending plates. The L-shaped brackets used to mount the cornice box on the wall will provide further support later.

STEP 2

3 Mark and cut a decorative edge or arch on the front piece, if desired. It's best to keep it simple. Use large sheets of newspaper to make a template.

Shape the lower edge of the front panel.

4 Use the four Homasote pieces as templates to cut the same shapes from the batting. Cut the batting for the top and front as one piece. Cut the batting for the sides ½ inch larger on two adjacent edges. Set the batting pieces aside.

5 Join the box front and top together using 1⅝-inch drywall or deck screws, then join the sides. When viewed from the front, the edges of the top and sides should not be visible.

COVERING THE BOX

1 Glue the batting pieces to the box using spray adhesive or a glue gun. Don't overdo the gluing; it is only a tacking procedure to secure the batting while the cornice box is being upholstered.

STEP 1

2 For the covering, cut a piece of decorator fabric that measures W plus 2 times D plus 6 inches long and L plus D plus 6 inches wide. If the box has a curved lower edge, measure from the longest point. You might wish to drape the fabric on

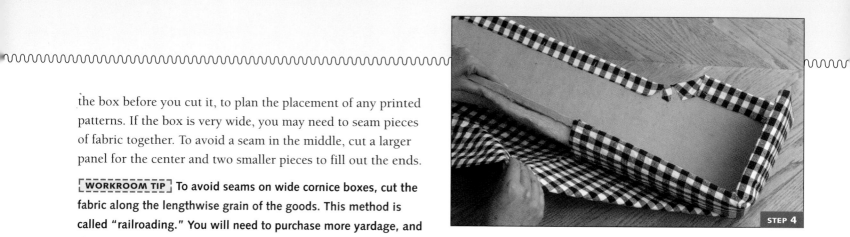

the box before you cut it, to plan the placement of any printed patterns. If the box is very wide, you may need to seam pieces of fabric together. To avoid a seam in the middle, cut a larger panel for the center and two smaller pieces to fill out the ends.

[**WORKROOM TIP**] **To avoid seams on wide cornice boxes, cut the fabric along the lengthwise grain of the goods. This method is called "railroading." You will need to purchase more yardage, and there usually is some waste.**

3 Lay the cut fabric piece wrong side up. Place the cornice box on it, the front panel facedown and aligned on any patterns in the fabric. Do a dry run of steps 3 and 4 on p. 117 before actually stapling the fabric in place. Begin by drawing the fabric to the inside front of the cornice box, smoothing it out, and stapling it in place. Clip into the fabric along the curves to within 1 inch of the Homasote fiberboard so that you can make a clean edge.

4 Next, draw the fabric onto the sides of the cornice box, keeping the fabric grain straight. Fold the excess fabric to the inside edges, and staple in place. Finally, draw the fabric over the top of the box, working from the sides in toward the center and making diagonal folds at the corners as if you were wrapping a package. When the box is mounted, these folds will be on top, facing the ceiling, and will not be visible.

5 Run a self-fabric or contrasting welt along the lower edge of the cornice front and sides. Staple the lip of the welt to the inside edge of the box.

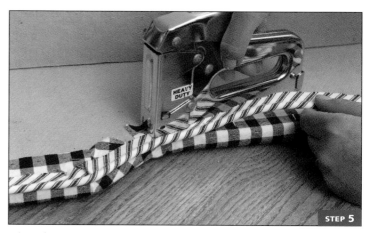

6 Finish the inside of the box with drapery lining. Staple it in place, smoothing and folding in the corners as you go. Glue on gimp to conceal the raw edges. Use clear-drying fabric glue such as Fabri-Tac®.

MOUNTING THE BOX

Mount the box above the window using L-shaped brackets. Choose brackets 1 inch shorter than the box depth (D) so that they will be hidden from view. Mount the brackets securely at the proper height on the wall, spacing them 20 inches apart. Set the cornice box on top of the brackets, and screw them to the inside top.

Mock Fan Shade

The mock fan shade is one of the easiest window treatments to create. The fan effect is created by looping a tab over the rod and scooping up fabric from the bottom of the shade. Sheer- to tapestry-weight fabrics are suitable. Since the fabric requirements are minimal, you might want to splurge on something expensive. The shade is lined, and a lining in a contrasting fabric can make a nice surprise when the shade is drawn up.

There are no drawstrings or shirring tapes here, just a self-fabric tab loop.

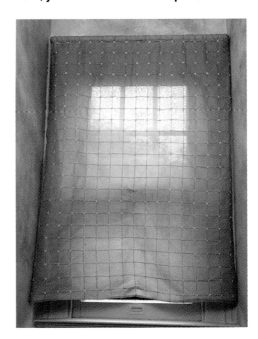

FOR ONE SHADE, YOU'LL NEED:

- Fabric for shade
- Fabric for lining
- Curtain or spring-tension rod
- Large button
- Measuring and marking tools
- General sewing/craft supplies

MAKING THE SHADE

1 Measure the window width and length. Purchase shade and
lining yardage 4 inches longer than the window length to
make a shade and matching tab. You can make the tab from the
shade fabric, the lining fabric, or another fabric.

2 Place the shade and lining fabrics right sides together.
Cut a rectangle 1 inch wider and 3 inches longer than the
window dimensions from the double layer. Do not separate
the layers.

3 Sew the two layers together along the two sides and one
bottom edge with a ½-inch seam allowance. Trim the
corners. This technique is called "pillowcasing."

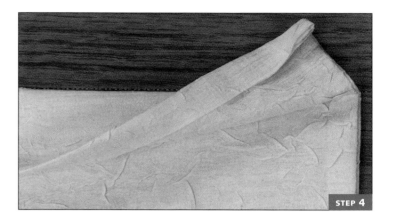

STEP 4

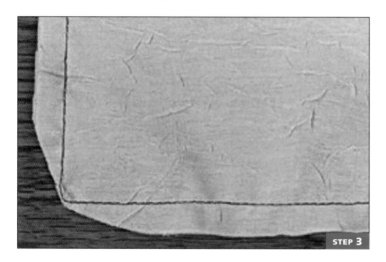

STEP 3

4 Turn the work right side out and press. Fold the top raw
edge ½ inch toward the lining and press. Fold again
1½ inches to 2 inches to form a casing for the curtain rod.
Topstitch in place. Mount the curtain on the rod.

MAKING THE TAB

1 For the tab, cut a strip of fabric 3½ inches wide by the
length of the shade plus 2 inches. The final length can be
adjusted later. Fold the strip in half lengthwise, right side in.
Sew across one short end and down the long edge with a ½-inch
seam allowance. Press the seam allowance back on itself to
facilitate turning. Trim the seam allowance to ¼ inch, and clip
the corners diagonally.

STEP 1

[WORKROOM TIP] Clear plastic curtain rods, available from
Kirsch®, are practically invisible when used with sheer fabrics.

DESIGN IDEA For a different look on a wider window, make two
tabs and position them 12 inches to 14 inches in from each side.

2 Turn the tab right side out, press well, and pound flat.
Loop the tab around the middle of the shade, up and over

TRICK *of the* TRADE

OPAQUE WINDOW WITH JAPANESE PAPER

Japanese paper admits lots of light while screening out a so-so view.

If you would like to mask an ugly view out a window or keep others from looking in without cutting down on the natural light, Japanese paper is the answer. Upscale paper stores carry these elegant handmade papers. Choose a paper that is not too heavy, to allow the light to enter. The sheet size must be 4 inches wider than your window. Some papers are very narrow and may not be suitable. For a wide window, you might substitute an interesting semisheer fabric that is 45 inches to 60 inches wide.

To mount the paper in the window, you will need a wooden frame sized to fit the window opening. Make it yourself from wood strips, or ask a frame shop to construct one for you. Have a ¼-inch-thick sheet of Plexiglas® cut to fit the window opening, and ask for predrilled screw holes in the corners (see TAP Plastics under Resources on p. 198). Screw the Plexiglas sheet to the frame.

Press the Japanese paper with a dry iron to take out any wrinkles. Lay the paper wrong side up on the floor. Lay the frame on top, Plexiglas side down. Wrap the paper around the edges and corners of the frame, and staple to the back. Screw magnets to the four frame corners and the magnet mates to the inside of the window. With the magnets in place, the frame can easily be put in and taken out of the window. If the window is in a stairwell, the frame can be removed temporarily when moving furniture in and out.

STEP 2

the rod, and pin the ends together. Decide how much of the window you want to reveal, and repin the tab accordingly. Unpin the tab, and trim off any excess. Fold in the raw edges at the open end of the tab, and stitch closed. Make a buttonhole 1 inch from the machine-sewn end, and sew a button to the other end.

3 Loop the tab around the shade once again, and button closed. Pleat the middle of the shade behind the tab so that the sides cascade down like fans.

DINING AND ENTERTAINING

Part 5

Entertaining involves your creativity every step of the way, from planning the menu to cooking to food presentation. Table runners, napkins, place mats, and tablecloths set the stage for all types of gatherings, from informal brunches to lively, elegant evenings. Even a buffet can be upscale with a silverware holder so beautiful that it becomes the focus of your table. Ordinary chairs become more festive with fabric covers sewn especially for parties. If you don't have a dining room, you can still entertain in style at a coffee table covered with a colorful oriental rug.

Round Tablecloth

I f you have a round table, you know how difficult it can be to find a round tablecloth you like in an affordable price range. By making your own table-cloth, you free yourself of that time-consuming search. In fact, once you learn the easy technique, you may never purchase a round tablecloth again.

Before You Begin see **Fabric Preparation** on p. 94.

FOR A ROUND TABLECLOTH, YOU'LL NEED:

- 54-inch-wide fabric
- Measuring and marking tools
- General sewing/craft supplies

Serge the edge of your tablecloth or make a folded hem. If you've never used your machine's blind hemmer, here's your chance to give it a try.

PREPARING THE MATERIALS

1. Use the Round Tablecloth Worksheet on p. 128 to determine the size of your tablecloth and the fabric yardage needed.

2. Preshrink the fabric, remove the selvages, and straighten the cut ends.

[WORKROOM TIP] Don't depend on plaids that are printed on the fabric for straight cutting lines—they may be printed off grain. A woven plaid is more reliable. To tell whether a plaid has been printed or woven into the fabric, check the back of the fabric. A woven fabric will look the same on the front and the back. A printed fabric will probably be white on the back.

MAKING THE TABLECLOTH

1. Cut the fabric in half crosswise. Cut one piece in half lengthwise. Seam the two narrower pieces to either side of the larger piece, right sides together and matching any pattern. Make sure napped panels all run in the same direction. Press the seams open. Instead of having one seam running down the middle, your tablecloth will have two seams and neither one will fall on the tabletop.

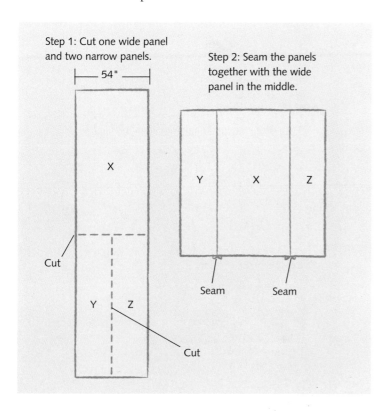

Step 1: Cut one wide panel and two narrow panels.

|— 54" —|

X

Cut

Y | Z

Cut

Step 2: Seam the panels together with the wide panel in the middle.

Y   X   Z

Seam   Seam

2. Fold the fabric in half, right side in, on a carpeted work surface. Fold once again into quarters. Run a pushpin through the end of a tape measure into the center point, pushing firmly into the carpet below. Hold the fabric marker against the tape measure at the point that is ½ your measurement D. For example, if D is 98 inches, you would hold the marker at 49 inches. Gently swing an arc across the fabric, marking as you go.

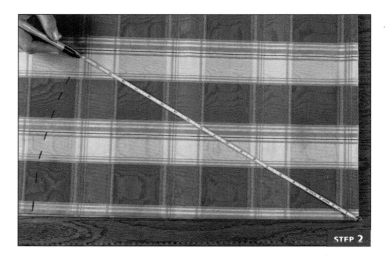

STEP 2

3. Cut along the marked line through all four layers, and open up the tablecloth. Serge the cut edge. Push on the back of the presser foot to draw up some of the fullness as you serge.

STEP 3

[WORKROOM TIP] While it may be tempting to make a round tablecloth out of a sheet, do this only if the table is purely decorative. Most sheets are not treated to be stain-resistant, and your food and beverage stains will become permanent.

TRICK
of the TRADE

WORKING WITH PLAIDS

Plaids can be used effectively in many home-dec sewing projects, from window treatments to tablecloths, if you know how to handle them. Here are a few pointers.

- There are two types of plaids: woven and printed. Problems arise with printed plaids when the design lines do not perfectly match the straight grain of the fabric. Such a plaid might work for a pillow but not for a window treatment. If you cut the curtain panels on grain, the plaid would look crooked. If you followed the plaid to cut, the panels would not hang straight.

- Plaids look more attractive if the hem fold is made on a dominant line of the plaid. If you are making curtain panels or a slipcover skirt, choose the location of the hem fold first. Then measure from there, adding the right amount of fabric below for the hem allowance and the right amount above for the panel length.

- Plaids should line up at the seams; even a little jog off register is distracting. For a perfect match, affix narrow double-sided zipper tape within the seam allowance of one piece. Peel off the paper backing.

- Fold and press the seam allowance of the second piece to the wrong side. Lay this fabric on top of the first piece, match up the plaids, and press gently to adhere.

- Fold both pieces right sides together, and stitch the seam. Peel off the tape, and press the seams open. The plaids will be perfectly matched across the seamline because the tape prevented the fabric layers from shifting.

4 Press the serged edge 2 inches to the wrong side. If the serging you did in step 3 did not draw in enough of the fullness to get a smooth flat hem, run an ease stitch around the edge with the conventional sewing machine. Blind-hem stitch, topstitch, or hand-sew in place.

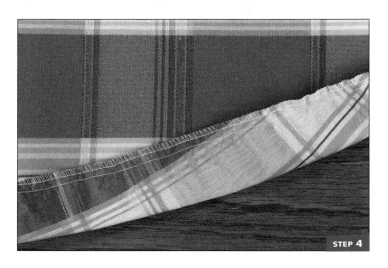

STEP 4

SCRAPS of Knowledge

STRETCH VELOUR

For an elegant tablecloth that needs no ironing, use stretch velour. Velour machine-washes and dries beautifully with absolutely no ironing. It does, however, experience progressive shrinking, which means that it shrinks again after a first washing. To overcome this, buy an extra ½ yard, and preshrink *twice* in a warm-water machine wash and permanent-press dryer cycle. A mere ½-inch allowance is needed for the hem. Serge ½ inch from the edge with woolly nylon thread, cutting off the excess velour as you go, to make a neatly rolled hem.

ROUND TABLECLOTH WORKSHEET

Use this worksheet to figure out the tablecloth fabric requirements for tables up to 48 inches in diameter. The tablecloth is designed so that no seams show on the tabletop.

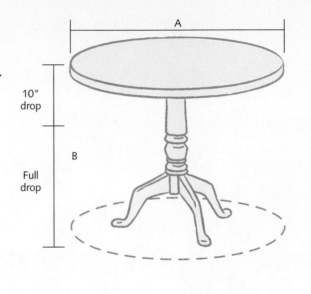

Fill in all the blanks in inches.

Diameter of the table   (A)_____

Length of the drop   (B)_____

Hem allowance   (C)_____

Fabric width (54" or wider)   _____

Pattern repeat, if any   _____

Finished tablecloth diameter: A + B + B   _____

Tablecloth diameter before hemming:

A + B + B + C + C + 2" seam allowance   (D)_____

The idea behind this design is to fit the tablecloth across two fabric widths. To verify that your tablecloth is not too big for the fabric, divide D by the fabric width and round up to the nearest whole number. Proceed if the result is 2. If the result is 3, see if you can tinker with your numbers. For example, if you serge the edge instead of folding a hem, those few extra inches that you gain might let you make the tablecloth in the size you want.

Fabric yardage required:

Multiply D times 2.   _____

Enter the pattern repeat, if any.   _____

Enter 18" (½ yard) to allow for shrinkage.   + 18"

Add the last three numbers together.   =_____

Divide the result by 36".   ÷ 36"

Enter the result. This is the final yardage needed.   =_____

Party Chair Back Covers

Few households have enough matching chairs to serve a crowd for dinner. The expense of buying extra chairs (and storing them) for one or two big family gatherings a year hardly seems worth the trouble. The catch is that once the table is set, the candles are lit, and the turkey is being carved, the mix-and-match look of assorted dining room and kitchen chairs is a distraction. If you know you will be giving big dinners at least a few times a year, why not make matching slipcovers for the chair backs? This project is not time-consuming or expensive since only the chair backs are covered. The covers can be as simple or as detailed as you want.

Two different chairs—one from the breakfast nook, the other from the dining room—get ready to host a big affair with matching chair back covers.

Before You Begin see **Single Welt** on p. 13 and **What Is Boxing?** on p. 50.

FOR EACH CHAIR BACK, YOU'LL NEED:

- Fabric for front/back
- Fabric for boxing strip and facing
- Fabric for bow (optional)
- Fabric and ¼-inch cord for welt
- Fusible fleece
- Lightweight fusible interfacing
- Muslin for patterns
- Measuring and marking tools
- General sewing/craft supplies

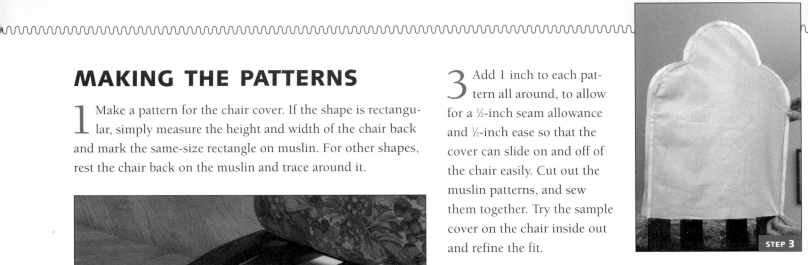

MAKING THE PATTERNS

1 Make a pattern for the chair cover. If the shape is rectangular, simply measure the height and width of the chair back and mark the same-size rectangle on muslin. For other shapes, rest the chair back on the muslin and trace around it.

STEP 1

3 Add 1 inch to each pattern all around, to allow for a ½-inch seam allowance and ½-inch ease so that the cover can slide on and off of the chair easily. Cut out the muslin patterns, and sew them together. Try the sample cover on the chair inside out and refine the fit.

4 If you want to add a bow to the cover, make a sample out of muslin, pin it to the chair cover, and mark the position.

2 Make a pattern for the boxing strip. For the strip width, measure the depth of the chair back. For the length, measure around the entire chair back, starting and ending at the seat edge and following all the contours. Add 2 inches for extra ease (any excess can be cut off later). Mark a strip this length and width on muslin.

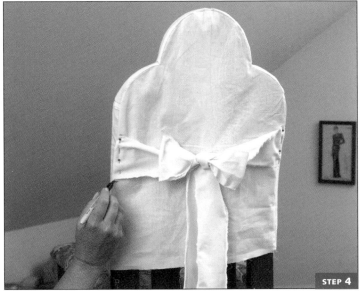

STEP 4

STEP 2

SEWING THE CHAIR COVER

1 Take the sample apart. Use the muslin pieces as patterns to cut two chair covers, one boxing strip, and four bow strips from the various fabrics for each cover you are making. The steps that follow are for one chair cover. If you are making multiple covers, you may want to proceed assembly line style, rather than making the covers one by one.

[WORKROOM TIP] If you are using a printed or patterned fabric, you'll want all the chairs in the set to look the same. Draw part of the design on the paper pattern so you can position it in the same spot on the fabric for every piece you cut.

2 To lightly pad the chair cover, cut two chair covers from fusible fleece and fuse them to the wrong side of the fabric pieces. Fuse lightweight interfacing to the boxing strip to stabilize it and give it body. You could also underline the strip with denim or duck.

3 Place the bow strips right sides together in pairs. Trim off one corner diagonally. Machine-stitch ½ inch from the edge all around, leaving the short straight end open. Clip the corners diagonally, turn right side out, and press. Pin the short raw end of each tie to the back cover, right sides together and raw edges matching, as marked on the muslin pattern.

4 Make covered welt twice as long as the boxing strip, using the ¼-inch-diameter cord and the contrasting fabric. Pin the welt to the outside edges of the front and back cover, right sides together; leave the bottom edge plain. Stitch together using a zipper foot so that you can get close to the cord. Pin the boxing strip to the back cover, right sides together, and stitch together, enclosing the welt and raw edges of the ties in the seam. Join the front cover the same way. Trim off the boxing-strip ends even with the chair cover bottom edge.

5 Measure the lower edge of the chair cover all around. Cut a facing strip 1 inch longer than this measurement by 3 inches wide. Join the short ends together with a ½-inch seam allowance. Press one long edge ½ inch to the wrong side and topstitch. Pin the facing to the lower edge of the chair cover, right sides together and raw edges matching. Stitch all around with a ½-inch seam allowance. Press the seam open, and then fold the facing to the inside of the cover. Hem or tack in place.

DESIGN IDEA To dress up the lower edge, enclose welt in the facing seam, too. This look is shown in the photo on p. 129.

Buffet Silverware Holder

Your buffet table can be as elegant as any sit-down dinner when you make a classy display of the silverware. This circular holder has room for 16 place settings of silverware. If your guest list is bigger, try putting a complete place setting in a single slot.

Fabric options for a silverware holder include silk organza, tapestry, velveteen, and linen. Avoid stretch velour or knits, which are difficult to stitch together in so many multiple layers.

FOR ONE SILVERWARE HOLDER, YOU'LL NEED:

- 1½ yards fabric
- 1½ yards contrasting fabric
- Beads or an appliqué
- Fusible interfacing
- Fabri-Tac fabric glue
- Measuring and marking tools
- General sewing/craft supplies

CUTTING THE FABRIC CIRCLES

1 For the first circle pattern, draw two 16-inch perpendicular lines that cross one another at the center, or 8 inches in from the ends.

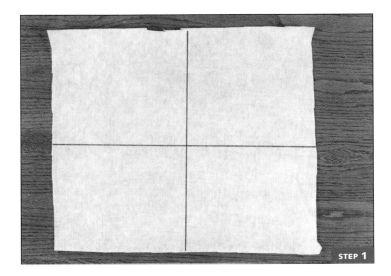

2 Fold the paper into quarters on the marked lines. Use a tape measure and a marker to swing an arc 8 inches from the center point across the top quadrant. Cut on the marked arc, and open out the 16-inch-diameter circle pattern.

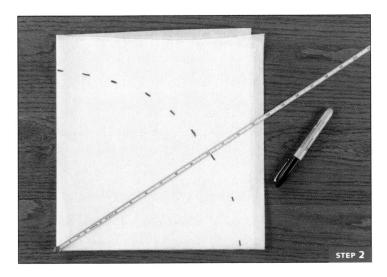

3 Repeat steps 1 and 2 to cut 20-, 24-, and 28-inch-diameter circle patterns. Layer the four patterns in order of size.

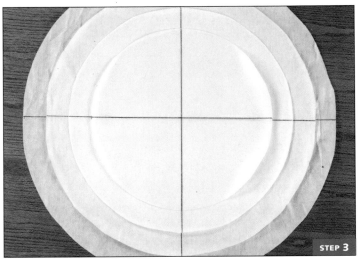

4 Cut two fabric circles for each pattern. Alternate the fabric colors for the progressive circle sizes.

SEWING THE HOLDER

1 Place each pair of circles right sides together. Machine-stitch ⅜ inch from the edge all around. Press the seam back on itself.

2 Cut a 3-inch slit at the center *through one fabric layer only.* Reach into the opening, and turn the circle right side out. Press well. Cut a 4-inch by 1-inch strip of fusible interfacing. Slip it under the slit, in between the fabric layers, so the fusible side faces up. Press again to fuse the slit closed. (If your fabric is sheer, eliminate the slit and leave a small opening in the circumference for turning instead.)

3 Stack and center the four circles according to size. Pin the layers to prevent shifting. Using chalk or an air-erasable marking pen, draw two perpendicular lines through the center, like those on your patterns, to divide the work into quarters.

STEP **3**

4 Using a wide, long zigzag or decorative stitch, sew along one line from edge to edge through all the layers. To sew the second line, start at the center and stitch out to the edge, first in one direction and then in the opposite direction. Stitch four more lines from the center out to the edge, dividing the work into eighths. Finally, stitch down each one-eighth wedge, dividing the work into sixteenths. You can mark the stitching lines or simply eyeball it.

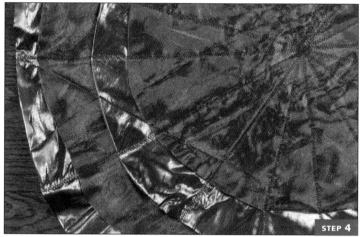

STEP **4**

5 Embellish the center of the circle by gluing on beads or a purchased appliqué.

6 To use the holder, put the spoons in the smallest circle, forks in the second circle, and knives in the third circle. The fourth, outer circle forms the base.

Elegant Table Runner

Table runners that combine fabrics and trims attract the most attention. Here, three silky fabrics are accented with textured braid. A cord around the outside edge frames the piece and also makes the seam easier to turn. A standard size for runners is 14 inches to 16 inches wide and 72 inches long, but you can tailor the measurements for your tabletop.

Arrange the runner in loose folds to create a sense of drama and opulence.

Before You Begin see **Decorative Cord Joins** on p. 137.

FOR A 72-INCH-LONG RUNNER, YOU'LL NEED:

- 1⅓ yards fabric for center panel
- 2 yards fabric for side panels and backing
- 1 yard fabric for end panels
- 5 yards decorative cord
- 1 yard flat braid
- 2 tassels (optional)
- Measuring and marking tools
- General sewing/craft supplies

MAKING THE PANELS

1 Prepare the fabric by cutting off the selvages and straightening the ends.

2 Cut a 12-inch by 48-inch center panel and two 4-inch by 48-inch side panels from your selected fabrics, the longer edges along the lengthwise grain. Join the side panels to the center panel on the long edges, right sides together, with a ½-inch seam allowance. Press the seams open.

3 For the end panels, cut two 18-inch by 16-inch pieces, the shorter edge along the lengthwise grain. To create a point on the end of each panel, find the midpoint of one long edge, measure ½ inch in from the edge, and make a dot. Make a dot on each short edge 4 inches from the corner. Draw lines connecting the three dots. Cut on the marked lines.

CREATING THE RUNNER

1 Pin each end panel to the center section, right sides together and raw edges matching. Stitch with a ½-inch seam allowance. Press the seams open.

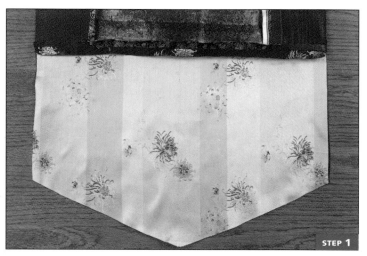

2 Press the work from the right side so the pieces lie flat and smooth. Topstitch decorative flat braid over each end-panel seam.

DECORATIVE CORD JOINS

Decorative cord is used to trim seams in pillows, duvet covers, upholstery, and table runners—any item where two fabrics are seamed together. Similar to welt, the cord has a woven tape, or lip, along one edge. The lip can range in size from ¼ inch to 1 inch wide. Since it is easier to sew with the edges matching, you may want to adjust the seam allowance on your project to match the width of the cord lip.

Narrow cords can be overlapped without creating excessive bulk, but thicker cords, ⅜ inch or more in diameter, require a different approach to avoid a large lump at the join. While the process is a bit tedious, the resulting join is barely discernible.

1 Measure the edge of the project piece all around. Cut the cord this length plus 6 inches, and tape the ends to prevent raveling.

2 Pin the cord to the edge of the fabric, leaving 3 inches of cord hanging free. Start in the middle of a long section where the join will most likely be hidden, such as the back of a cushion or the bottom of a pillow; never start at a corner.

Use a zipper foot to stitch the cord all around, clipping into the lip of the cord as needed to turn corners or provide ease around the curves.

3 Stop sewing when you are 1½ inches from the starting point. On the free ends, pick out the stitches that hold the cord to the lip. Immediately wrap the ends of the cords with clear tape so that they will not unravel.

4 Trim the lip so that the ends overlap by 1 inch, and pin or staple together, keeping free of the fabric. Retwist the individual cords one by one, using the memory of the fibers, and slip them under the lip.

5 Do the same for the remaining pieces. Arrange the cords so half of them fall under the lip and half fall on top.

6 Arrange all the cords in a single layer. Complete the stitching line along the tape to hold them in place.

3 Sew decorative cord to the runner, ½ inch in from the edge, using a zipper foot. Clip into the lip to provide ease at each corner; you can even push the cord together a bit as you round the corners to help the finished work lie flat. When you reach the starting point, overlap or join the ends, depending on the cord construction. Press the corded edges flat.

STEP 3

[WORKROOM TIP] If the fabric begins puckering as you sew on the cord, stop and evaluate the situation. See if you can press out the puckers. If this doesn't work, hand-baste the cord to the fabric edge and then resume the machine sewing.

4 Lay backing fabric right side up on a flat surface. Place the front panel on it, right sides together. Cut backing fabric to match the front panel. Pin together in the seam allowance all around. Machine-stitch through both layers over the previous stitching with a zipper foot, leaving a 6-inch opening in one side for turning.

STEP 4

DESIGN IDEA Whenever possible, make your table runners and place mats reversible. The amount of extra work is minimal and you end up with two items almost for the price of one. If both sides are pieced together from various fabrics, make sure the seams line up to avoid a seam imprint when the runner is pressed. This is especially important with thin fabrics, such as silk.

5 Press the seam allowance from the underside of the runner back on itself. Trim off the corners of all seam allowances. Reach through the opening, and turn the runner right side out. Hand-stitch the opening closed.

6 Cover the surface of the runner with a press cloth. Press well, pounding the edges flat with a tailor's clapper for a professional finish. Hand-sew a tassel to each pointed end, if desired. Be sure to remove the tassels before dry-cleaning the piece.

Place Mats and Napkin Holders

Place mats don't take long to make, and if you choose beautiful fabrics, your end product will rival any place mat you see at any price. This design uses two different fabrics, one for the insert and one for the backing and mitered border. The backing/border fabric is cut in one piece, which gives the edges a neat, trim look and makes the miters incredibly easy to sew. Use fabric left over from another project to make the decorative napkin holders.

The grass cloth insert fabric is from Poppy Fabric; see Resources on p. 198.

FOR FOUR PLACE MATS AND NAPKIN HOLDERS, YOU'LL NEED:

- 1 yard 25-inch-wide grass cloth for insert
- 1¼ yards silk brocade fabric for backing/border
- ¼ yard fabric or scraps for napkin holders
- Measuring and marking tools
- General sewing/craft supplies

MAKING THE PLACE MATS

1 Cut four 12-inch by 18-inch pieces from the grass fabric and four 16-inch by 22-inch pieces from the silk brocade.

[WORKROOM TIP] Rectangular place mats can be made in any size, not just the standard 12 inches by 18 inches. Cut the fabric for the place mat insert the desired finished size. Cut the backing/edging fabric 2 inches larger all around than the desired finished size. Once you know the sizes to cut, you can figure out how much fabric to buy.

2 Lay each silk brocade piece right side up. Draw a chalk line 2 inches in from each edge. Press each edge ½ inch to the wrong side. Then fold in and press on the chalk lines.

3 Fold in each corner diagonally, lining up the crease lines. Press to set the diagonal crease.

4 Refold each corner in half, right side in, aligning all the pressed-in folds exactly. Pin the layers together to prevent any shifting. Using small stitches, stitch slowly and accurately along the diagonal crease.

5 At each corner, trim off the excess fabric ¼ inch beyond the stitching line. Press the seam open from the wrong side. Turn the miter right side out, and push out the corner with a point turner. Press well.

6 Trim down the grass fabric insert about ⅜ inch or to a size that can be slipped under the mitered border easily, without pulling or buckling. The exact amount to trim will depend on the fabric thicknesses. Slide each insert in place.

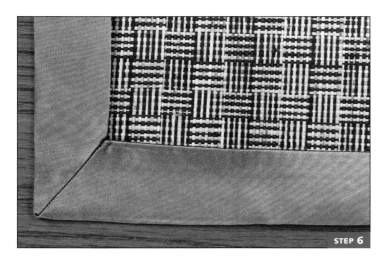

STEP 6

7 Topstitch the inner border edges all around, securing all the layers. Using a decorative stitch makes an attractive look for the underside and will make the place mat reversible.

STEP 7

[WORKROOM TIP] Keeping place mats clean is always a challenge. To remove silk brocade from the luxury category, prewash it by machine in warm water and machine-dry on a permanent-press cycle. It will lose about 10 percent of its sheen in the process but be more practical for place-mat use. Treating the grass cloth/silk brocade combination on both sides with Scotchgard spray will allow these surfaces to be wiped off with a damp cloth.

MAKING THE NAPKIN HOLDERS

1 To make a pattern, draw a triangle on paper (graph paper is useful for this) that is 4 inches wide at the base and 11 inches tall. Cut out the pattern, and trim 1 inch off the top point. Use the pattern to cut two matching or contrasting pieces of fabric for each napkin holder desired.

STEP 1

2 Place the fabric pieces right sides together in pairs. Using a small stitch length, machine-stitch all around with a ¼-inch seam allowance, leaving a 2-inch opening at the base. Hand-walk two diagonal stitches at each corner.

3 Press back the seam allowances. Trim the corners diagonally. Turn each piece right side out. To help turn the points, slip a needle with a double thread into the stitches, and pull both ends of the thread. Press the point well. Press the raw edges at the base ¼ inch to the wrong side. Hand-sew the opening closed. Press the entire piece.

4 Make a 1-inch-long buttonhole in each piece, centering it ¾ inch in from the base of the triangle. Cut the buttonhole open.

STEP 4

5 To form the napkin ring, pull the narrow end through the buttonhole.

STEP 5

DESIGN IDEA One advantage to making your own place mats is that you're not limited to traditional shapes or sizes. On this set, tapered curves allow the four place mats to fit comfortably on a small round table without any overlapping corners. The edges are bound with Wrights® double-fold bias quilt binding. See the Faux-Fur Throw instructions on p. 76 for the binding technique.

Napkin Finishes

apkins are so easy to make. The three finishes shown here have three different personalities. The serged edge makes up the fastest and is perfect for everyday napkins; just avoid loose weaves to prevent serging that works loose and pulls off the edge. The double-rolled hem is tailored and practical. For your most elegant table settings, there is the mitered-corner hem. Mitered hems look best ironed, so if you are the "I hate to iron" type, choose one of the other finishes instead. Napkins must be cut on grain or they will not be square after the first washing. Start out by straightening the ends of the fabric.

Medium-weight linen makes the nicest napkins. Cotton damask and good-quality medium-weight cottons that press well are also good choices.

Before You Begin see **Fabric Preparation** on p. 94.

FOR A SET OF NAPKINS, YOU'LL NEED:

- Medium-weight fabric, all-natural or a blend
- Measuring and marking tools
- General sewing/craft supplies

MAKING A SERGED-EDGE NAPKIN

1 Cut one square of fabric for each napkin, the same size as (or a fraction larger than) the desired finished size.

2 Set your serger for a rolled hem, making the stitches very close together. Tighten the lower looper so that the hem will roll. Stitch along the edge all around. At each corner, serge off the end, pull the thread off the stitch fingers, turn the corner, and sew the next side.

MAKING A DOUBLE-FOLDED HEM

1 Cut one square of fabric for each napkin, 1 inch larger than the desired finished size.

2 Press each edge of the square ½ inch to the wrong side. Turn one raw edge under until it meets the inside fold and pin. The result is a ¼-inch double roll. Stitch along the second foldline. Repeat to hem the opposite edge. Then hem the two remaining edges.

MAKING A MITERED-CORNER HEM

1 Cut one square of fabric for each napkin, 4 inches larger than the desired finished size. For a 20-inch dinner napkin, you will need a 24-inch square to start.

2 Press each edge of the square ½ inch to the right side. Fold each edge 1½ inches to the right side, and press to set the crease. Open out the fold.

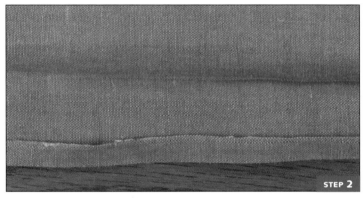

3 Fold in each corner diagonally, wrong side in, lining up the crease lines. Press to set the diagonal crease. Refold each corner in half, right side in, aligning all the pressed-in folds exactly. Pin the layers together to prevent any shifting. Using small stitches, stitch slowly and accurately along the diagonal crease.

4 Trim off the excess bulk at each corner. Turn the corners right side out, and press the edges and corners all around. To finish, topstitch the folded edge with a straight needle, or sew a decorative hemstitch using a winged needle (Wing 100/16), which goes into the same hole more than once, to pierce tiny holes that become visible when the napkin is held up to the light. Linen and organza look especially pretty when stitched this way. If the wing needle doesn't pierce clear holes, apply spray starch to the fabric to stiffen the fibers. Press well when finished.

STEP 4

DESIGN IDEA To make napkins with a contrasting mitered border, see the Faux-Fur Throw instructions on p. 76. Cut the binding 5 inches wide from a compatible fabric.

SCRAPS *of* Knowledge

NAPKIN SIZES

Finished napkin sizes range from a 9-inch-square cocktail napkin to a 20-inch-square dinner napkin. How big to cut the initial square depends on the edge finish you choose. For a serged edge, the square is cut to the finished size; for a rolled edge, 1 inch larger; and for a mitered-corner edge, 4 inches larger.

One approach, of course, is simply to decide on the number of napkins to be made, their finished size, and the type of hem and figure the yardage requirements from there. A more economical approach is to consider the width of the fabric and tweak your other numbers. For example, if the fabric is 45 inches wide after the selvages have been removed, you can cut three 15-inch squares across the width. If you hem with a serger or make a narrow double-fold hem, you end up with napkins that are adequate but not overly generous. For a larger napkin, you might want to start with 60-inch-wide linen fabric instead. You can still cut three squares across, but they would measure 20 inches instead of 15 inches. A narrow hem on these squares would make a nice-size 19-inch napkin. For a mitered-corner hem without fabric waste, 45-inch-wide fabric is a good choice. You can cut two 22-inch squares across the width and end up with an 18-inch-square napkin after hemming.

Rug-Covered Coffee Table

On your last visit to your parents' house, as you poked around the attic, looking for hidden treasures, you noticed a fairly decent oriental rug. Closer inspection turned up several worn spots as well a major hole. If the rug was in perfect shape, you would feel guilty about cutting it up, but in its current condition, it might be an item to recycle into a covering for a coffee table or large floor pillows. If the rug is big enough, you can do both.

Choose a low table with simple lines for your project. If you don't already own a suitable table, you can pick up one at an unfinished-furniture store or IKEA.

FOR ONE TABLE, YOU'LL NEED:

- Parsons style coffee table
- A rug to sacrifice
- 1-inch-thick batting
- Heavy-duty staple gun with ⅜-inch staples
- Upholstery tacks and hammer (optional)
- Double-ended screws (optional)
- Scotchgard spray
- Sharp heavy-duty scissors
- Pliers
- Staple remover
- Measuring and marking tools

PADDING THE TABLE

1 Turn the table on its side, unscrew the legs, and set them aside. (If the legs do not unscrew, you will have to work around them.) Mark the screw holes on the underside of the tabletop.

2 Roll out enough batting to cover the tabletop and wrap around to the underside. Turn the table upside down on the batting, and trim away the excess batting about 4 inches beyond the table edge all around. Wrap the batting around one long edge of the table. Staple it to the underside at 4-inch intervals, about ½ inch from the batting edge.

STEP 2

3 Fold over and staple the other long edge of the batting, as you did in step 2. At the short edges, start at the middle and work out. When you reach the corners, staple the batting to the edges of the table, instead of the underside, and trim off the excess. Trim out the batting around the screw holes where the legs will be reattached.

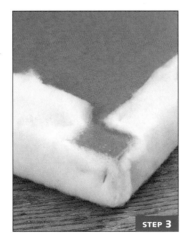

STEP 3

4 For each leg, cut a piece of batting the exact length of the leg and the exact measurement to go around the leg once. Staple the batting down one side of the leg. Wrap the batting once around the leg, butt the edges when you reach the starting point, and staple in place.

STEP 4

ATTACHING THE RUG

1 Roll out the rug, and identify a section in good condition to use for the tabletop. Turn the rug facedown, and place the tabletop, batting side down, on the selected spot. Staple in a few places, just enough to secure the rug to the tabletop temporarily. Turn the assembly over, and check the placement of the rug pattern. Adjust as needed.

2 When you are satisfied with the rug placement, turn the entire assembly facedown. Cut away the excess rug about 5 inches beyond the table edge all around. Fold both long edges of the rug onto the underside of the tabletop and staple in place, just as you did for the batting. Remove the temporary staples.

3 At each corner, fold in the remainder of the long edge and staple down. Trim out the area around the screw hole, and staple down the cut edges. Trim out the portion of the long edge that falls beyond the tabletop and extends over the adjacent edge. Work slowly, taking care not to trim out too much. Fold in the adjacent edge on an angle.

STEP 3

4 Bring the angled edge up and onto the underside of the tabletop, and staple securely. Staple the complete short edge of the rug in place, from corner to corner. Make sure each corner edge is covered and stapled securely.

STEP 4

5 For each leg, cut a piece of rug large enough to wrap once around the leg plus 1 inch and to extend ½ inch beyond the leg at each end. Lay each piece wrong side up. Fold in the short edges ½ inch, set the table leg on top, and anchor one long edge with a few staples. Wrap the rug around the leg, keeping the short edges on the ends of the legs folded in as you go. When you reach the starting point, fold in the long edge about ¾ inch, overlap the first edge, and staple down through the triple layer.

STEP 5

[WORKROOM TIP] If your staple gun will not go through thick layers of carpet, use upholstery tacks instead, tapping them into place with a hammer. You may prefer upholstery tacks to staples along the leg seam for a nicer finished look.

6 Use pliers to untwist the leg screw a bit, or replace it with a longer screw, in order to reattach the leg over the excess bulk. Screw each leg into the tabletop, with the stapled seam toward the inside.

STEP 6

7 Spray the top of the table with Scotchgard to protect the surface from spills.

Decorative Fireplace Screen

Without a roaring fire, a fireplace adds little to a room's decor and often ends up a black hole. Making your own fireplace screen can provide a decorative focus and help you pull the look of the room together. This project requires no sewing, just a staple gun and some fabric glue. The overall size and number of panels is based on the size of the fireplace and the width of the fabric you choose to cover the screen. This screen can be made larger for a room divider, too.

FOR ONE FIREPLACE SCREEN, YOU'LL NEED:

- Homasote fiberboard
- Fabric for front of screen
- Fabric for back of screen
- Medium-weight quilt batting or fleece
- ½-inch-wide gimp trim
- Two 2-inch-long by ½-inch-wide metal hinges for each panel join
- ⅞-inch-long screws
- Staple gun and ½-inch-long staples
- Fabri-Tac fabric glue
- Small pruning saw
- Spray adhesive
- Measuring and marking tools

Decorative fireplace screens are not widely available, but it's quite easy to design and make your own.

149

GETTING STARTED

1 Measure the height of the fireplace opening and add 4 inches for measurement A. Measure the width of the opening and add 8 inches for measurement B. Jot down your figures. Your finished freestanding screen needs to measure at least A tall by B wide to cover the opening.

2 Decide whether to make a three- or a five-panel screen (always choose an odd number of panels so that there is a panel in the middle). Also decide whether you want all the panels to be the same width—an arrangement that looks especially nice in a five-panel screen—or if you would like the middle panel to be larger. Use a calculator to work out panel widths that add up to B. For example, if B is 50 inches, you might decide on a 26-inch-wide middle panel flanked by two 12-inch-wide side panels. If the fabric is 54 inches to 60 inches wide, there will be no problem cutting all three of these pieces across one fabric width.

3 Mark a pattern for each panel on newspaper, using the sizes you decided on in steps 1 and 2. The top edges can be left straight or rounded off, as you choose. Keep the shaping simple so the panels don't become difficult to cut out or cover with fabric. Headboards might give you some ideas for this silhouette. Cut out the paper patterns. Fold the patterns in half, and trim as needed to true up shapes that are symmetrical.

ASSEMBLING THE SCREEN

1 Lay the panel patterns on Homasote fiberboard and trace around the outline. Use a ruler to mark straight lines. Cut out each panel on the marked line using a small pruning saw. Work outdoors or in a garage because this step is messy. The building supply store where you bought the Homasote fiberboard may be equipped to cut out the panels for you.

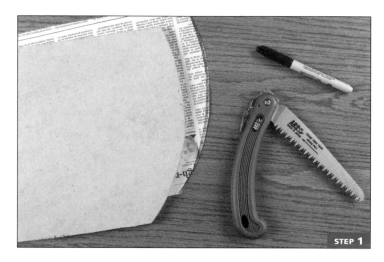

STEP 1

2 Lay each pattern on the backing fabric, and cut out each panel 1 inch beyond the edges all around. Cut the fabric for the front of the panels the same way. Cut two pieces of fleece for each panel to pad the front and back.

3 For padding, apply spray adhesive to each Homasote panel, one side at a time, and affix the fleece to it. Trim off any fleece that extends beyond the panel edges.

STEP 3

4 Lay one panel wrong side up. Lay the backing fabric on top, right side up. Starting at the middle of one edge, wrap the fabric onto the edges of the panel, and staple into the edge to hold it in place. Then pull the fabric taut and staple the opposite edge. Do the same for the other two edges. Continue in this way, working from the middle out to the edges, alternating sides and pulling the fabric taut and even as you go. When you reach the corners, make sharp, flat folds and staple down. If your fabric is thick, you might want to trim out some of the bulk on the corners. Repeat for all the panels.

6 Lay the panels facedown, side by side, on a flat surface. Hinge the panels together along the side edges, using two hinges per join and spacing the hinges 6 inches from the top and bottom edges of the screen. Use ⅞-inch drywall screws instead of the screws packaged with the hinges, in order to pass through the fabric layers into the Homasote. To finish, glue gimp around the side and top edges of each panel, covering the staples and raw edges.

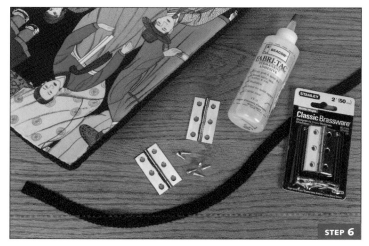

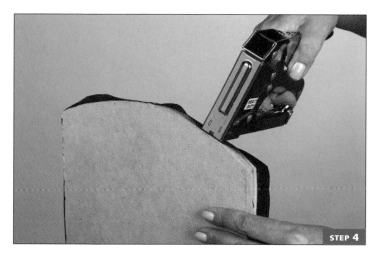

STEP 4

[WORKROOM TIP] Fabri-Tac is a quick-drying fabric glue suitable for many fabric projects. It dries quickly, is clear and washable when dry, and remains supple.

5 Repeat the stretch-and-staple technique from step 4 to cover the front of the panels. Remember to confine the stapling to the edge of the panels. The raw edges will be covered with gimp later.

STEP 5

Part 6 PILLOWS

Of all the home-dec projects in this book, pillows may become your favorite. They provide options for every room in the house, from fur pillows for your bedroom to a TV pillow to hide the remote control. Pillow fabrics can run the gamut from silk brocade to tapestry. You will learn how to use shirring, ruching, and tufting to create special effects, when and how to put in a zipper, and even how to cover a pillow with no sewing at all. You'll also discover that not all pillows are square. Pillow forms in nontraditional shapes make for fun projects, and creating custom-made patterns to cover them is not hard. You can even make pillow fronts out of ribbons.

Television Remote Control Pillow

I f the remote controls for the TV are frequently misplaced at your house, this handy pillow might be the answer. Keep this pillow on the couch, and get the controls off the coffee table where space is usually at a premium. The technique for designing and sewing the faced shapes can be used to add pockets to other pillows as well.

PREPARING THE PIECES

1 Cut two 10-inch by 14-inch pieces of paper. Use one piece as a pattern to cut one pillow front and one pillow back from the appropriate fabrics. Set the fabric pieces aside.

[**WORKROOM TIP**] When you need to make paper patterns for small squares and rectangles, use graph paper. The lines on the graph paper can act as both a ruler and a cutting line, enabling you to cut your patterns to the precise measurements required.

2 Draw two curving lines freehand across one pattern for the pocket edges, dividing the rectangle roughly into thirds (see the photo at left). Make the lower pocket at least 5 inches deep, to hold your remote securely. A gentle curving edge will let the pillow accommodate remotes of different sizes. Avoid extreme curves, which will not turn well.

3 Hold both pieces of paper together, and cut ¼ inch above the top-pocket line through both layers. Separate the papers and cut ¼ inch above the bottom-pocket line through one layer only. Discard the scraps, leaving two pocket patterns. Cut one pocket front, one lining, and one fleece for each pattern.

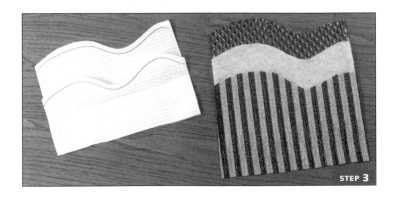

STEP 3

FOR A TELEVISION REMOTE CONTROL PILLOW, YOU'LL NEED:

- 10-inch by 14-inch pillow form
- ½ yard fabric for pocket fronts and pillow back
- Small piece of contrasting fabric for pocket linings
- Small piece of fabric for pillow front
- ½ yard fleece
- Measuring and marking tools
- General sewing/craft supplies

SEWING THE PILLOW

1 Place the lower pocket front and lining right sides together, the lining on top. Slip the fleece layer underneath. Using small stitches, machine-stitch along the curved edge with a ¼-inch seam.

2 Trim the seam allowance to ⅛ inch, and clip the curves. Open up the pocket, and finger-press the seam allowance toward the bottom edge. Fold back the lining, letting it extend ⅛ inch above the seam to create a piping effect. Pin in place. Cover the pocket with a press cloth and press lightly, to set the crease. Remove the pins and press again, firmly, until the piece is flat. Repeat steps 1 and 2 to make the upper pocket.

3 Lay the pillow front right side up. Position the upper pocket on it, right side up, aligning the lower edges. Next, overlay the lower pocket, also aligning the lower edges. Pin in place and then hand-baste. The pillow front now has two pockets for remote controls and a copy of *TV Guide®*.

4 Place the pillow front and pillow back right sides together. Machine-stitch around the side and bottom edges, and sew 2 inches past each corner on the top edge, using a ½-inch seam allowance. Clip the corners, and turn right side out. Press the seam allowances on the open edge ½ inch to the inside. Insert the pillow form, and slipstitch closed.

Striped Ribbon Pillow

A ribbon pillow can be a work of art. The stripes in this pillow are actually short lengths of ribbon, joined edge to edge over a backing. You can collect your ribbons over time, buy them all at once, or do a combination of these two approaches. Vintage stores can be a good source for ribbons that are too short for other purposes. Look for interesting woven-in patterns, and vary the surface textures, from flat to high sheen. If you fall in love with a ribbon that is ultra expensive, add some plainer ribbons to the mix, both to set off the pillow and to keep the cost reasonable. Strips of silk brocade fabric can also be worked into your design.

Using faux fur for the pillow back produces a pelted effect along the side seams.

FOR ONE PILLOW, YOU'LL NEED:

- Assorted ribbons
- Scraps of silk brocade
- Square pillow form
- Faux-fur fabric for pillow back
- Medium-weight fusible Pellon interfacing
- Sulky KK 2000 Temporary Spray Adhesive
- Measuring and marking tools
- General sewing/craft supplies

GETTING STARTED

1 Measure the pillow form from seam to seam in both directions, without crushing the loft. Draw a square 1 inch larger than this measurement on medium-weight fusible Pellon interfacing. Cut out the square.

2 Cut the assorted ribbons into pieces slightly longer than one edge of the square. Lay the ribbons edge to edge on a flat work surface, rearranging them until you have a sequence that you like. Continue cutting and placing ribbons until you have enough to cover the entire square. You can also use strips of silk brocade in your design, but be sure to place a ribbon on either side to overlap and cover the raw edges of the fabric. Choose wide ribbon or fabric strips for the two outer edges, which include a ½-inch seam allowance.

[WORKROOM TIP] If the project is to be washed or dry-cleaned, make sure that all of the materials used can be cleaned in the same manner. Trim that must be dry-cleaned should not be added to a pillow you plan to wash. Ribbons shrink in water but not from dry cleaning.

MAKING THE PILLOW

1 Protect your ironing board surface with a large sheet of tissue paper. Place the interfacing square on the tissue, fusible side up. Spray lightly with fusible adhesive, just enough for a temporary hold. Begin transferring the ribbons one by one, in sequence, to the interfacing square. Butt the edges of the ribbons so that no interfacing shows through. Overlap the raw edges of the fabric strips with ribbon. After you have positioned several ribbons, cover them with a press cloth and press lightly with a warm iron to fuse in place, just to make a temporary bond. If any ribbons do not bond, pin them in place instead. Repeat until the entire square is covered.

[WORKROOM TIP] Overlap the ribbons if necessary to keep them running parallel to the edges of the square. Antique ribbons, in particular, may have irregular edges that can skew the lines off course.

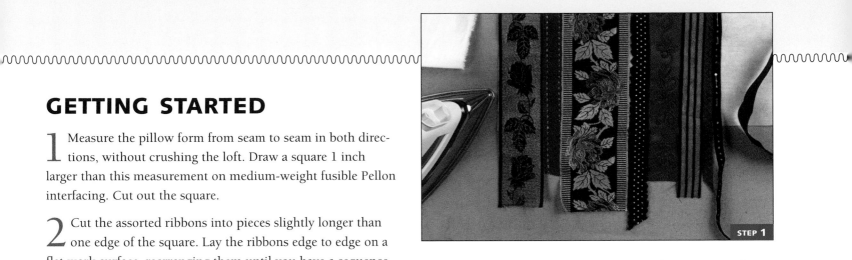
STEP 1

2 Set the machine to a 3.0mm zigzag or decorative stitch. Using matching or contrasting thread, sew over the butted or overlapped edges through all layers. Change the top thread color as needed. Variegated threads work well here.

STEP 2

3 Turn the work wrong side up. Trim off the ribbon ends even with the edge of the interfacing square. Use the square as a template to cut a matching piece from faux fur for the pillow back. Place the pillow front and back right sides together. Machine-stitch around three sides and 2 inches past the corners on the fourth side, using a ½-inch seam allowance. Clip the corners, and turn right side out. Insert the pillow form, and slipstitch closed.

[WORKROOM TIP] If you make a lot of pillows, cut large plastic squares in assorted sizes to use as templates. The see-through templates make it easy to center a design and cut with a rotary cutter. Sheets of ³⁄₁₆-inch-thick template plastic are available from TAP Plastics (see Resources on p. 198).

TRICK
of the TRADE

DECORATIVE PILLOW FRONTS

If you look closely at pillows in expensive shops, you will notice that the construction is often quite simple: a pillow front, a pillow back, and maybe some braid around the perimeter. The pillow may have a zipper opening or buttons on the back, but more often than not, the edges are simply whipstitched together along one side. So why are these pillows so expensive? The pillow front is miniature work of art. Here are two design ideas for your next pillow.

Design Idea One: Shirring

In this design, the pillow front is divided into thirds, and the middle section is shirred. Satin is a good fabric choice for this treatment because of the way the shirred section catches the light.

1 Measure your pillow form, add a ½-inch seam allowance all around, and make a pattern. Use the pattern to cut the pillow back. For the front, draw two lines on the pattern dividing it in thirds. Cut the pattern apart. Mark an X along each cut edge as a reminder to add a ½-inch seam allowance.

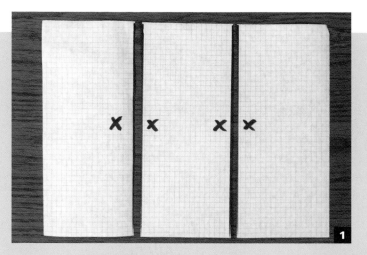

2 Use each side-panel pattern to cut a piece of fabric with the added seam allowance. For the middle panel, cut a piece 1 inch wider than the pattern (to allow for two seam allowances) and three times as long. Zigzag over a thin piece of string within the seam allowance along both long edges.

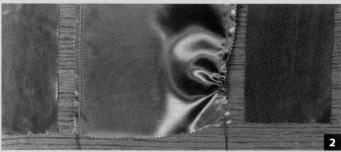

3 Pull up the strings to gather the edges of the middle panel to the pattern length. Place the middle panel on a side panel, right sides together, and sew a seam along the gathered edge. Join the other side panel the same way. Complete the pillow assembly as usual.

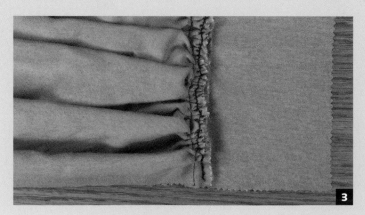

Design Idea Two: Faced Openings

Faced window openings add a new and unusual dimension to a pillow front.

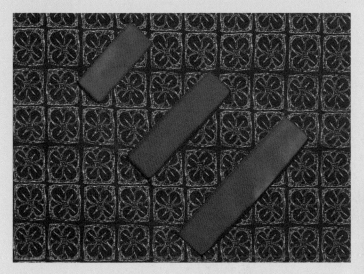

1 Measure the pillow form, add a ½-inch seam allowance all around, and make a pattern. Use the pattern to cut one pillow back, one front, and one front lining, to peek through the window openings.

2 Cut a paper template for each opening you desire, experimenting with different sizes and shapes. Lay the pillow front facedown, and arrange the templates on the wrong side, spacing them at least 3 inches apart. Another idea is to place a single template in the center. Trace around each template with a fabric-marking pen.

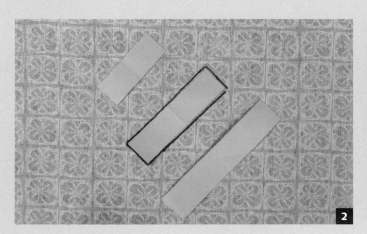

3 Place the templates on a new piece of fabric. Cut 1 inch larger all around each one to make the facings.

4 Position the facings on the pillow front, right sides together, to correspond to markings on the reverse side. Hold the fabric up to a window so you can see the marks. Pin close to the facing edges through both layers.

5 Set the machine to a short stitch length. Stitch from the wrong side on the marked lines, hand-walking two stitches diagonally at each corner to facilitate turning. Cut down the middle of each facing and diagonally out to each corner.

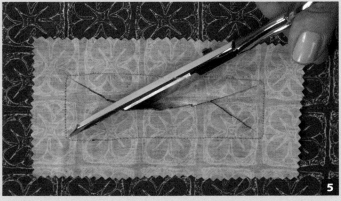

6 Turn each facing to the wrong side of the pillow front. Press well on both sides. Topstitch to hold the facings in place. Layer the pillow front over the contrasting lining and baste around the edges. Complete the pillow assembly as usual.

Flange Pillow

The flange pillow is a dramatic look, with no zipper to clutter up its clean lines. It can be made in any size and just about any fabric for use on a bed or couch, or even as an oversized floor pillow. Leather, suede, rubber, satin brocade, velveteen, and traditional decorator fabrics are all possibilities. The 20-inch square pillow shown here features a 3-inch flange, for a finished size that is 6 inches larger than the pillow form. On the back, two overlapping pieces provide the opening for inserting and removing the pillow form.

Don't make a flange too wide or the fabric will get floppy.

FOR ONE FLANGE PILLOW, YOU'LL NEED:

- Square pillow form
- Fabric for pillow cover
- Measuring and marking tools
- General sewing/craft supplies

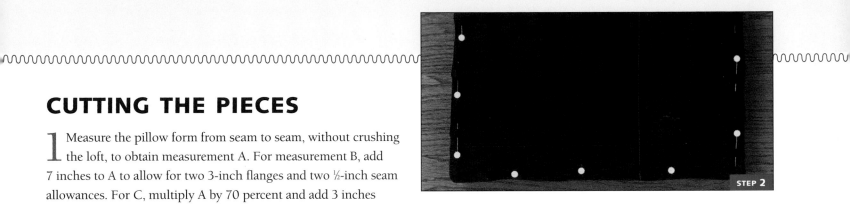

CUTTING THE PIECES

1 Measure the pillow form from seam to seam, without crushing the loft, to obtain measurement A. For measurement B, add 7 inches to A to allow for two 3-inch flanges and two ½-inch seam allowances. For C, multiply A by 70 percent and add 3 inches (the flange width). You can round up C to the nearest inch. Jot down all your figures. You can use these formulas to calculate A, B, and C for various sizes of square pillows and flange widths.

2 Cut out two patterns for your flange pillow cover from newspaper: a square that measures B by B for the pillow front and a rectangle that measures B by C for the pillow back.

3 Use the patterns to cut out one front and two backs from fabric. The 20-inch-square pillow shown required 1½ yards of 45-inch-wide fabric. A 36-inch-square pillow with a 3-inch flange, to use as a floor pillow, requires 3 yards of 45-inch-wide fabric. Use your patterns to figure out how much fabric you will need.

SEWING THE FLANGE COVER

1 Serge one B edge of each pillow back. Press the serged edge 3 inches (or one flange width) to the wrong side to form a hem. Stitch in place.

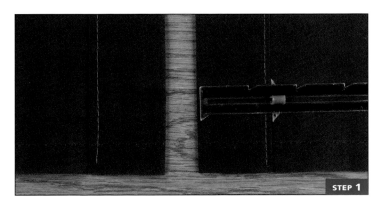

2 Lay the pillow front right side up on a flat surface. Place one pillow back on top, right side down, matching three raw outer edges. The hemmed edge will reach about two-thirds across the pillow, leaving the remaining one-third of the pillow front exposed. Position the second pillow back on top, right side down, to cover the exposed section. The two hemmed edges will now overlap at the middle. Pin the edges together.

3 Machine-stitch ½ inch from the edge all around. Trim the seam allowances to reduce bulk. Trim the corners diagonally. Reach through the back opening, and turn the pillow cover right side out. Press well, especially the outside edges.

4 Measure 3 inches in from the outside edges all around, and mark with an air-soluble marking pen or a marker appropriate to your fabric. Using a single or a double needle, stitch on the marked line all around through both layers to form the flange. Insert the pillow form through the opening at the back.

[WORKROOM TIP] Never use waxed chalk to mark silk. It will leave stains.

SCRAPS of Knowledge

FLANGES

A flange is a flat, decorative edge of fabric that extends beyond the soft cushiony part of the pillow. Only the crispest, firmest fabrics will produce a flange that can stand up on its own. Other fabrics need some sort of stabilizer—either fusible interfacing, for a crisp effect, or fusible batting or fleece, for a soft effect. The stabilizer will change the hand and often the appearance of the fabric, so it's important to use it for the entire pillow, not just the flange, for the application to succeed.

Neck Roll

The ends of this bolster shape are cinched and tied off.

A neck roll can be an aid for sleeping if you have neck problems, but its use is not limited to the bedroom. The small rolled shape can add a nice accent to your living room decor, tucked in between the seat and arm of a sofa or placed across the back of a chair.

Before You Begin see **Making Bias Tape** on p. 25.

FOR ONE NECK ROLL, YOU'LL NEED:

- 14-inch by 5-inch pillow form
- ⅝ yard fabric for middle section
- ⅝ yard fabric for extensions and ties
- ¼ yard fabric for contrasting trim
- Measuring and marking tools
- General sewing/craft supplies

MAKING THE PILLOW COVER

1 Cut the main pillow pieces. For the middle, cut a 13-inch by 19-inch piece. For the extensions, cut two 4-inch by 18¾-inch pieces. Serge each piece all around the outside edge.

2 Press both short edges of each extension ⅜ inch to the wrong side and topstitch. Press one long edge 1 inch to the wrong side and stitch to form a casing.

STEP 2a

STEP 2b

3 Cut two 20-inch by 1¾-inch strips from the trim fabric, either on the crossgrain or on the bias, piecing as necessary. Fold each trim strip in half lengthwise, wrong side in, and press to set the crease. Pin the trim strips to the middle section along the long edges, right sides together. Let the ends extend evenly at each end. Sew together with a ½-inch seam allowance, taking care not to stretch the fabric. Trim to even up the ends.

STEP 3

4 Pin the extensions to the middle section, right sides together, sandwiching the trim in between. Let the middle section extend ½ inch at each end. Stitch together over the previous stitching. Fold the work in half, right side in, and pin the edges of the middle section together to form a tube. Stitch together with a ½-inch seam allowance. You don't need to sew the extensions.

STEP 4

MAKING THE TIES

For the drawstring ties, cut two 30-inch by 1½-inch strips. Press the long edges ¼ inch to the wrong side, by hand or with a bias-tape maker. Then fold in half, and press again to make a ½-inch-wide strip. Sew close to the folded edge through all thicknesses, tucking in the ends. Use a safety pin to draw a tie through each casing. Insert the pillow form into the cover, centering it between the two extensions. Pull the drawstrings to gather the extensions, and tie closed.

[WORKROOM TIP] To make your own neck roll pillow form, roll up batting or use a roll of paper towels (remove the plastic wrapper).

SCRAPS of Knowledge

SILK FABRIC LUXURY

Silk dupioni and silk taffeta make stunning accent pillows. These fabrics should not be used for upholstery or seat cushions, however, because they are too fragile to handle the excessive stress on the seams. Silk should also be kept away from direct sun to prevent fading and deterioration. If you have difficulty finding silk fabrics in your area, Thai Silks offers items through mail order.

ODD-SHAPED PILLOWS

Pillows come in many terrific shapes and sizes to spark your creativity. To cover an odd-shaped pillow, you must first make a pattern. This sounds a lot harder than it really is. Use the seams of the pillow form to define the shapes of the pattern pieces you'll need. Read through all instructions since the method for making the patterns differs from shape to shape.

Down and feather pillow forms come in
all shapes and sizes . . .

. . . and make
unique pillows.

For a cube-shaped pillow, set the pillow form on paper and trace the shape outline. Add a ½-inch seam allowance all around.

For a sphere-shaped pillow, drape a piece of muslin on the pillow form (muslin will conform better than paper to the curved surface). Hold in place with pins. Pinch each side of the muslin near the middle of the pattern piece, forming small ¼-inch darts. Tape the darts in place. Trace the seamlines from the shape onto the muslin.

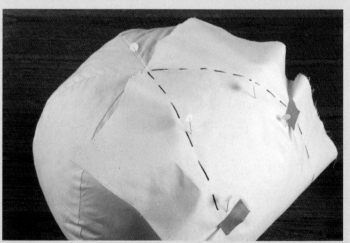

Unpin the muslin and cut out the shape on the marked lines, leaving the taped darts intact. Smooth the muslin over your home-dec fabric to use as a template. You can add a ½-inch seam allowance for a loose fit or no seam allowance for a snug fit.

The pieces in a sphere-shaped pillow are apt to meet in an imperfect join, but this is the perfect spot for a button embellishment, to hide any imperfections and give the ball some definition.

Odd-shaped pillow forms really strut their stuff when made with multiple fabrics. Brocades and velvets can be stunning. Avoid plaids for cone-shaped pillows; the match at the seam will look awkward.

For a cone-shaped pillow, wrap a piece of muslin around the pillow form. Mark a line where the fabric meets itself, add a ½-inch seam allowance, and trim off the excess. Then trim off the excess around the bottom edge.

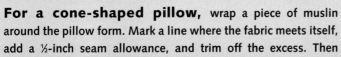

Trace around the base of the cone and add a ½-inch seam allowance to make a circle pattern for the base. Sew the cone seam. Insert four pins evenly spaced around the edge of the cone and the edge of the base. Then match up the pins to sew the pieces together.

Fur Pillow with Inset

This pillow is based on the simple idea of cutting out two identical shapes from contrasting fabrics and then using one cutout to fill in the hole left by the other. When the fabric is fake fur, the seams are easily camouflaged. Simple shapes make the best insets. When you find a motif you like, enlarge or reduce it on a photocopier to a size you can use. You can also fold scrap paper in half or quarters to cut your own design.

A stylized diamond inset looks as if it was always part of the red fur fabric.

FOR ONE PILLOW, YOU'LL NEED:

- Square pillow form
- Faux fur for pillow front and back
- ¼ yard of a contrasting fur for the inset
- Small sharp scissors
- Soft toothbrush
- Fabric glue
- Beeswax
- Measuring and marking tools
- General sewing/craft supplies

MAKING THE INSET

1 Trim the selvages off the faux fur. Measure the pillow form from seam to seam, and add 1 inch. Cut two squares from the faux fur to these dimensions for the pillow front and back.

[WORKROOM TIP] Faux fur comes 62 inches to 64 inches wide. This generous width allows you to cut a pillow front and back, each measuring up to 30 inches square, from just under 1 yard of fabric. You can make two fur pillows that size from the same yardage—just cut the pillow backs from another fabric, such as cotton velveteen.

2 Choose a simple geometric shape or design for the inset, or create your own by folding a piece of paper in half or quarters and cutting a symmetrical shape. Transfer your design to cardboard, and cut it out to make a sturdy template for tracing. Mark a dot in the center. Add a few lines perpendicular to the edges to help with matching (similar to notches on a dress pattern). Draw an arrow to indicate the direction of the fur nap.

STEP 2

3 Lay the fur for the inset facedown on a flat work surface, noting the nap direction. Place the inset template on top, making sure the nap arrow runs the same way. Trace around the outer edge of the template using a felt-tip marking pen, a sliver of soap, a chalk pencil, or whatever shows up best on the knit fur backing. Choose a marking tool that makes a thin line, for accurate cutting later. Add the other template markings as well.

4 Lay the pillow front fur side down on the work surface, noting the nap direction. Locate the center of the square, and mark it with a dot. Place the inset template on top, matching the center dots and observing the nap direction. Trace around the template once again, as you did in step 3.

5 Using very sharp scissors, cut out both pieces on the marked lines. Use only the points of the scissors, and cut through the knit backing only. Do not cut the fur hairs, as they will help fill in the edges later.

STEP 5

6 With the pillow front still fur side down on the work surface, drop the contrasting fur inset into the cutout opening. Be sure to observe the nap direction on both pieces, and line up the match points. Thread a needle with a double thread, run it through beeswax to strengthen it, and press the thread to set the wax. Whip the cut edges together, spacing your stitches $\frac{1}{4}$ inch apart and grabbing about $\frac{1}{8}$ inch of the fur backing from each side. Push the hairs out of the seam and toward the fur side of the pillow as you sew. Your goal is to make both furs lie flat. As you work around the shape, the open section may seem larger, even though you know they were cut exactly the same size. Simply use the needle and thread to pull in the cut edges of the opening to meet the edges of the inset. If the inset seems a bit big in a spot, trim the inset, not the opening, to avoid distortion.

STEP 6

7 Stabilize the join by applying a little fabric glue over the stitches on the wrong side. Let dry. On the right side, brush the fur gently with a soft toothbrush to fill in the area where the furs are joined.

STEP 7

SEWING THE PILLOW

1 Place the pillow front and back right sides together. If you are unable to hold the heavy layers together with oversize pins, use paper clips or clothespins. Push the fur toward the center of the pillow away from the seam allowances.

2 Machine-stitch the edges together with a ½-inch seam allowance, flattening each side of the seam as you sew to keep both pieces the same size. Stitch around three sides and go 2 inches past the corners on the fourth side. Hand-walk 3 stitches diagonally at each corner to give the corners room to turn. Clip the corners diagonally.

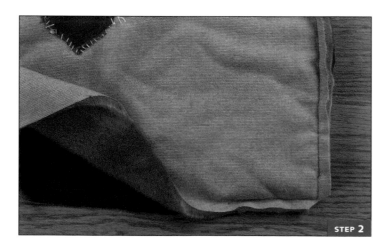

STEP 2

3 Turn the pillow cover right side out. Insert the pillow form. Hand-sew the opening closed. Use the point of a knitting needle to release the fur hairs that are caught in the seam. Brush the edge with a soft toothbrush to camouflage the seam.

SCRAPS of Knowledge

PILLOW FORMS

Pillow forms can be used over and over again. A good quality form—for which you pay a higher price—will last and keep its shape practically forever.

Two different fills are available: 100 percent polyester and a 95 percent feather/5 percent down combination. Feather and down pillow forms mold around your body and are very comfy and soft but must be shaken and fluffed back to their original shape afterward. The 100 percent polyester forms are often full in the center and empty in the corners. It is not possible to squish the filling into the corners with the cover intact. To get at the filling, open a side seam about 5 inches or big enough to get your hand in. Firmly push some polyester into each of the corners, remove a handful of the filling from the center, and then resew the opening. Adjusting the fullness in this way will make the pillow resemble the more expensive feather and down pillow form, but it still won't feel like one.

Picture Frame Pillow

The picture frame pillow lets you highlight a particularly beautiful piece of fabric or embroidery, just as a gallery frame shows off a painting. Any image that is printed or painted on fabric can be used. The frame opening has a facing of sheer organza, which minimizes the bulk. Additional organza can be layered on top of the image to soften the colors. The pillow shown here has a traditional look, but there's no reason to stop there. The window opening can be a circle or oval, a triangle, or a free-form shape. Have fun creating these small works of art!

Before You Begin see **Single Welt** on p. 13 and **Ruched Welt** on p. 171.

FOR A PICTURE FRAME PILLOW, YOU'LL NEED:

- Fabric with image to be framed
- Square or rectangular pillow form larger than image
- Decorator fabric for pillow front and back
- Metallic silk organza fabric
- Sheer fabric and ¼-inch cord for ruched welt
- Measuring and marking tools
- General sewing/craft supplies

The construction technique allows the frame to lie flat against the pillow front.

CUTTING THE PIECES

1 Measure the pillow form length and width, from seam to seam. Add 1 inch to each measurement. Cut two pieces of fabric to these dimensions for the front and back of the pillow. Cut a piece of organza the same size for the facing.

DESIGN IDEA If you like soft pillows, cut the pillow front and back exactly 1 inch bigger than the length and width of the pillow form to allow for a ½-inch seam allowance all around. If you like a firmer pillow, cut the pillow front and back the exact size of the pillow form, without adding anything extra. Sew these covers together with a ½-inch seam allowance as usual. When you stuff the pillow form inside, the fit will be nice and taut.

2 Measure the length and width of the design you wish to frame. Add 1 inch to each measurement to determine the size of the window opening, and jot down your figures. This window will be ½ inch larger than the image all around. You can make the opening larger or smaller than this, of course, depending on what portion of the image you want to frame.

3 Mark the frame outline, centered, on the organza facing. An easy way to do this is to mark two sets of parallel lines that intersect. Lay the marked organza on the pillow front, right sides together.

SEWING THE PILLOW COVER

1 Using small stitches, sew on the inside marked line through both layers, hand-walking two small stitches diagonally at each corner for easier turning.

2 Using sharp scissors, cut diagonally from the middle to each corner through both layers.

[**WORKROOM TIP**] Fragile fabrics like metallic organza will snag unless you use a new 70/10 HM needle when machine sewing.

3 To form the window, turn the organza facing through the opening to the wrong side. Press well so that the facing is not visible around the edges of the window opening when viewed from the right side.

4 Position the window piece over the fabric with the design. For a muted look, cut a second piece of organza and slip it in between, over the design.

5 To secure the layers, lift up the frame fabric, one side at a time, and pin down the triangular flap underneath. Stitch down each flap over the previous stitching. Press the framed area. Trim off the excess flap if it is particularly bulky.

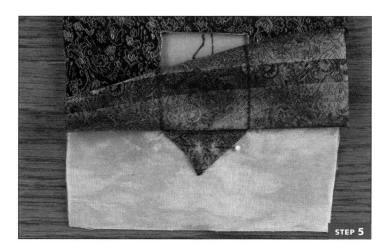

STEP 5

6 Use the sheer fabric and cord to make a length of ruched welt to go around the edge of the pillow front. Sew the welt around the edge of the pillow front, right sides together, and butt the cord ends together.

[WORKROOM TIP] Don't always do the predictable. Experiment with nontraditional trims such as fur strips, chenille fringe, and feathers for eye-catching trim.

7 Place the pillow front and back right sides together. Machine-stitch around three sides and 2 inches past the corners on the fourth side, using a ½-inch seam allowance. Clip the corners, and turn right side out. Insert the pillow form, and slipstitch closed.

RUCHED WELT

A ruched welt is similar to a single welt, except the fabric covering is shirred on the cord, lending a lush, elegant appearance. To make a ruched welt, cut the fabric strips on the straight grain three to four times longer than the cord, depending on the sheerness of the fabric, and ⅛ inch to ¼ inch wider than for a single welt. To begin, fold the strip over the cord, and secure the end with a safety pin. Stitch the edges together about ⅛ inch from the cord. After you have stitched a few inches, pull the cord toward you to shirr the fabric. Continue until you have shirred the required length.

SEWING ZIPPERS INTO SEAMS

Just as it is easier to insert a zipper into a dress before the shoulder and side seams are sewn, it is easier to insert a zipper in a pillow or cushion seam with the pieces lying flat. You can do this for a plain seam or a seam that has a welt.

Pillow back   Pillow front

Plain Seams

1 Machine-baste the pillow front and back together along one edge only. Press the seam open. Position the zipper facedown on the seam. Use narrow double-sided tape, sold in notions departments, to attach the zipper tape to the seam allowance.

2 Sew the zipper in place from the right side of the fabric. To avoid a dimple around the zipper pull, stop with the needle in the down position a bit before you reach this bulky area. Pick out a few of the basting stitches, and unzip the zipper for a few inches to pull the tab out of the way.

3 Complete the sewing. The stitching line should be even all around.

Welted Seams

1 To start, cut out the pillow front and back as usual, except use a 1-inch seam allowance on the edge where the zipper will be installed. Sew the welt or decorative cord to the pillow front as you normally would, except make the stitching line 1 inch in from the "zipper" edge.

2 Cut a length of a zipper 2 inches shorter than one edge of the pillow front. Bar-tack both ends. Close the zipper, and place it right side down on the edge of the pillow front, setting the zipper teeth firmly against the lip of the cord. Stitch alongside the zipper teeth through all the layers, starting and stopping 1 inch from each end of the zipper.

3 Fold the corresponding edge of the pillow back 1 inch to the wrong side, and press to set the fold. Place the back on the front, right sides together and raw edges even. Sew the pieces together along the pressed foldline just at the ends, from the corner to the zipper. You can't sew too far because the zipper gets in the way. Keep both 1-inch ends of the zipper free of stitching.

4 Open out the pillow front and back flat, right side up. The pressed fold on the back cover now meets the corded seam. Topstitch the zipper in place from the right side of the pillow back. Use tape if it helps you maintain a straight sewing line. If you want the zipper to be barely visible, use clear thread.

Jumbo Bolsters

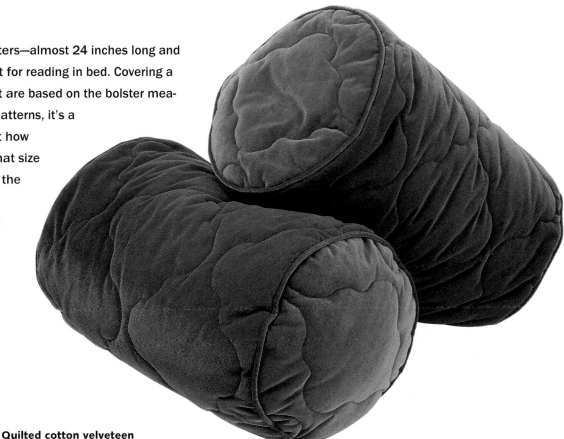

Giant feather and down bolsters—almost 24 inches long and 16 inches across—are great for reading in bed. Covering a bolster requires two patterns that are based on the bolster measurements. Once you make the patterns, it's a pretty simple matter to figure out how much fabric you will need and what size zipper to buy. You can even bring the patterns with you to the fabric store. These jumbo bolsters each took 1½ yards of 54-inch-wide fabric.

Quilted cotton velveteen fabric makes jumbo bolsters extra plush and soft.

Before You Begin see **Single Welt** on p. 13 and **Sewing Zippers into Seams** on p. 172.

FOR EACH BOLSTER, YOU'LL NEED:

- Bolster form
- Quilted velvet fabric
- Zipper
- Fabric and ¼-inch cord for welt
- Quilter's basting gun (useful with thick fabrics)
- Measuring and marking tools
- General sewing/craft supplies

CUTTING THE PIECES

1 Measure the bolster without crushing the loft. For measurement A, hold the tape measure across the end of the bolster at the widest part, from seam to seam. For B, measure the bolster length from seam to seam. For C, measure around the bolster. Jot down your figures for A, B, and C.

STEP 1a

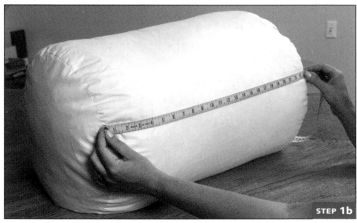
STEP 1b

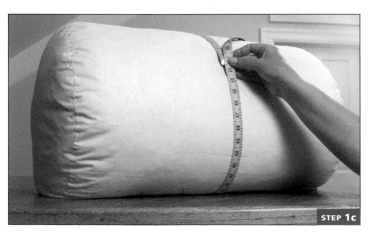
STEP 1c

WORKROOM TIP Don't rely on the bolster's hangtag measurements. These manufacturer's measurements do not take into account the loft of the pillow. When you are designing a cover, you should take your own set of measurements to be accurate.

2 Draw two patterns for your bolster cover on newspaper: a circle with measurement A as the diameter and a rectangle that measures B by C. Add 1 inch all around each piece for a ½-inch seam allowance plus ½-inch extra ease. Cut out both patterns.

3 For each bolster, you will need to cut two circles and one rectangle from fabric. Use your patterns to figure out how much fabric you will need. For large bolsters, you'll also need a zipper that is 3 inches shorter than the B edge of the rectangle.

4 Lay the fabric right side up. Place the patterns on top, centering the quilting design. Cut out two circles and one rectangle for each bolster. Machine-stitch the pieces ¼ inch from the cut edges to contain the loft.

SEWING THE BOLSTER COVER

1 Make enough covered welt cord to go around each fabric circle. Sew the welt in place, clipping into the lip to provide ease. Butt and join the ends.

SCRAPS of Knowledge

CUSTOM-QUILTED FABRICS

Decorator fabrics can be professionally machine-quilted for about $30 a yard from a workroom associated with Calico Corners. You can choose from several different quilting designs as well as a batting loft of 7 ounces or 10 ounces. The 7-ounce weight is fine for pillows; you might choose the 10-ounce batting for a puffy bedspread. The quilted fabric is returned to you with the decorator fabric on one side, drapery lining on the other, and the batting sandwiched inside. If you want to make a reversible spread, you can provide fabric for the underside as well, to be used instead of the drapery lining. The fabric length and width will each measure about 10 percent smaller after quilting, so plan accordingly.

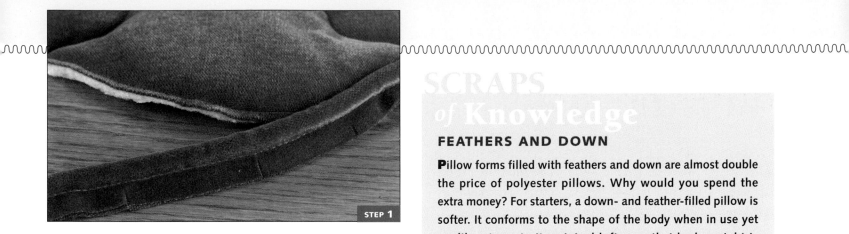

STEP 1

2 Fold the rectangle in half, right side in, and hand-baste the
B edges together with a ¾-inch seam allowance to form a
tube. Machine-stitch the seam at each end for 1½ inches only.
Hand-baste a zipper along the basted section of the seam. Topstitch in place.

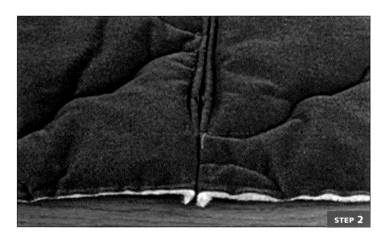

STEP 2

3 Remove the zipper-seam basting stitches, and unzip the
zipper about halfway. Turn the tube wrong side out. Pin a
fabric circle to each end, right sides together. A quilter's basting
gun can be used more successfully than pins to compress and
hold the multiple layers.

STEP 3

SCRAPS of Knowledge

FEATHERS AND DOWN

Pillow forms filled with feathers and down are almost double
the price of polyester pillows. Why would you spend the
extra money? For starters, a down- and feather-filled pillow is
softer. It conforms to the shape of the body when in use yet
readily returns to its original loft once that body weight is
removed. But not all down and feathers are created equal.

Feathers come in a variety of grades, defined by size and
quality. By separating the feathers and the down out of a mix,
a manufacturer can differentiate the feather qualities. Down,
the feathery covering found on the underbelly of a duck or
goose, is the finest and softest with the best fill power. The
second highest grade is "small feather," a light, fluffy premium feather with fill power second only to down.

The origin of the duck or goose, its diet, and weather condi-
tions all influence the quality of the loft. The finest down and
feathers come from Europe and Asia. Some down and feather
products found on the shelves are imported as finished
goods. Domestic producers import the feathers and then
wash and sort them for a superior finished product. This
cleaning is critical, as it rids the feathers of dirt, dust, and
naturally occurring oils that can cause allergic reactions. A
good-quality product is cleaned twice in special disinfectants
to prevent bacteria, yeast, mold, and odors from forming;
rinsed for 30 minutes until the water runs clean; and steam-
dried, resulting in curled feathers that are soft with high fill
power. Rub your fingers together on an end of the pillow. If
the feathers have not been properly cleaned, you will feel a
gritty substance, which is dirt falling off feathers.

Typically, feathers and down are used in combination, from
50 percent feather/50 percent down for a bed pillow to 95 percent feather/5 percent down for a decorative pillow. The
higher the feather ratio, the firmer the feel. Ideally, the feathers
will be small enough that you cannot feel the quills. A quick
check of the label will tell you the down/feather ratio as well
as the origin of the feathers and the place of manufacture.

4 Join the circle ends to the bolster, using a zipper foot to
sew in close to the welt and ease around the curves. Turn
the cover right side out. Open the zipper all the way, insert the
bolster form, and zip closed.

Tufted Pillow

Tufted pillows can add an unexpected design element to a pillow grouping. Use a solid-color fabric to best show off the dimples that are repeated across the surface. Tufting is also popular for seat cushions, as it compresses the inner filling without diminishing its softness.

Before You Begin see **Foam Cushions** on p. 45.

FOR A TUFTED ACCENT PILLOW, YOU'LL NEED:

- 14-inch square cut from 1-inch-thick foam
- ½ yard fabric
- ½ yard bonded polyester batting
- Quilter's Basting Gun by Dritz®, or long needle and embroidery floss
- Measuring and marking tools
- General sewing/craft supplies

Tufting produces a gently puckered tactile surface that invites touching.

MARKING AND CUTTING

1 For the tufting template, mark a 16½-inch square on a large sheet of paper, and cut out. Fold the square in half diagonally in both directions, and mark the center point. Measure out from the center point along each diagonal foldline and mark new points 4 inches apart.

2 Fold the paper square in half horizontally and vertically, making sure each fold passes through the center point. Mark a point on each of these foldlines 3 inches in from the outside edge. There should be 13 points in all.

3 Use the paper template as a pattern to cut two 16½-inch squares from the pillow fabric and two from bonded polyester batting. Trim down the batting pieces so that they are 16 inches square.

4 Pierce a small hole through each point marked on the paper template. Lay each fabric square right side up, place the template on top, and use an air-soluble marking pen to make a small dot on the fabric at each hole.

COMPLETING THE PILLOW

1 Place the pillow front and back right sides together. Machine-stitch around three sides and 2 inches past the corners on the fourth side, using a ½-inch seam allowance. Clip the corners.

2 Center and sandwich the foam between the two layers of batting.

3 Turn the pillow cover right side out. Fold the foam/batting sandwich in half, and insert it in the pillow opening. Relax the fold, letting the sandwich open up, and adjust the cover around it. Slipstitch the opening closed.

STEP 3

4 Tuft the pillow at each dot with the Quilter's Basting Gun or by hand. If you are making a lot of pillows, use the gun to save time. Follow the manufacturer's instructions, using the marked dots as entry and exit points. To tuft by hand, thread a long needle with embroidery floss to match the fabric. Draw the needle through to the right side, hiding the thread tail in between the layers. Tack the layers together securely at each marked dot. End off.

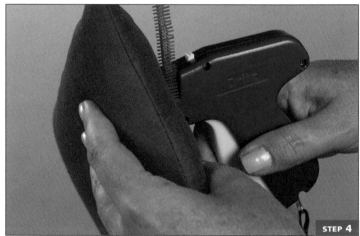

STEP 4

SCRAPS of Knowledge

QUILTER'S BASTING GUN

A quilter's basting gun is commonly used in drapery workrooms to help secure long side and bottom hems in place before stitching. You'll find many uses for this versatile tool in home-dec projects that require basting, tufting, or quilting.

TRICK
of the TRADE

NO-SEW PILLOW

You don't even need to get out the sewing machine for this one. All you need is a great piece of fabric twice the size of your pillow form. To cover a 20- or 22-inch-square pillow form, you'll need 1¼ yards of 45-inch-wide fabric. To cover a 26- or 28-inch-square form, you'll need 1⅝ yards of 58- to 60-inch-wide fabric. *Furoshis,* large fabric squares used by the Japanese to wrap presents, are terrific for this project.

Lay out the fabric square wrong side up on a flat surface. Lay the pillow in the middle of the square, in a diagonal orientation. Start by bringing two opposite corners of the fabric toward the middle of the pillow form, and tie them together.

Then bring the two remaining corners together at the middle, and tie them together. Tuck in the ends of the ties and any loose edges so that no part of the pillow form is visible.

Part 7

OUTDOORS

If you like to sew, then chances are you also like to garden. The patio or deck immediately outside your back door is an extension of your home, and you can use your sewing skills to make this area as individual as your home's interior decor. Everyone with outdoor furniture needs to replace the chair pads from time to time. Learn how to make a pattern for these pieces, and you can make new pad covers in a fabric that you choose. Create some shade by making an awning supported by lightweight polyvinyl chloride (PVC) pipes. Protect your expensive barbecue with a water-repellent cover. Then make a matching vinyl tablecloth to go over your umbrella table for those summer weekend brunches in the garden.

Awning

You can make your own awning for a fraction of what it would cost to buy one. All you need are Sunbrella® fabric and PVC pipes for the hidden framework. Kate Hamilton from Canvas Works in Middletown, California, has her awning frames professionally welded from 1-inch metal pipes and elbow joints. PVC pipes and elbows, which you can assemble yourself by hand, are a lighter-weight alternative.

Two fabric widths sewn together make a long striped awning to go over sliding-glass doors.

FOR A 6½-FOOT AWNING, YOU'LL NEED:

- 2½ yards 54-inch-wide Sunbrella fabric
- Two 10-foot-long ¾-inch-diameter PVC plastic pipes, schedule 40
- Four PVC plastic pipe elbows
- One 8-foot-long ½-inch-diameter electrical metallic tubing
- Two 8-foot-long 1¼-inch-diameter wooden dowels
- 1 package Kirsch metal pole brackets
- Two 8-inch by 8-inch flower pots filled with rocks
- Measuring and marking tools
- General sewing/craft supplies

Pipes, elbows, and brackets are some of the items needed for this project.

GETTING STARTED

1 Install two Kirsch metal pole brackets over the doorway, window, or other area where the awning will be mounted. It is preferable to screw them into a wood frame. Space the brackets no more than 48 inches apart, to support the awning weight evenly.

2 For the awning frame, cut each 10-foot PVC pipe into one 76-inch piece and one 33-inch piece. Also cut a 76-inch piece of electric tubing, to fit inside and support one of the PVC tubes. Use a pipe-cutting tool or ask the hardware store to cut the pieces for you. Set these pieces aside.

3 Cut the awning fabric 43 inches by 85 inches. The longer length will run parallel to the house. If your fabric is striped on the lengthwise grain, cut two 46-inch squares instead and arrange them side by side so that the stripes run as shown in the photo. Serge the edges together with a ½-inch seam allowance, trimming off the excess as you go. Serge the outside edge all around.

[**WORKROOM TIP**] Use polyester thread to sew the Sunbrella fabric. Cotton thread will eventually fade and rot after long exposure to the sun.

MAKING THE AWNING

1 Lay the fabric wrong side up on a flat surface. Fold in each corner by 7 inches, measuring along the straight edge.

2 Fold in each straight edge 3½ inches and press. Stitch ¼ inch from the serged edge all around to form a casing for the PVC poles.

STEP 2

3 Fold one long edge of the awning fabric in half and mark the center. Measure the distance between the mounted brackets. Make two corresponding marks on the awning edge, evenly spaced on either side of the center. At each mark, make a 2-inch-long buttonhole, parallel to and 2 inches in from the edge, for mounting the awning. Reinforce the ends of each buttonhole with small triangles of fabric.

STEP 3

STEP 1

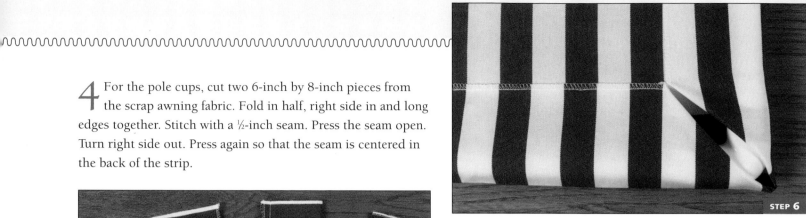

STEP 6

4 For the pole cups, cut two 6-inch by 8-inch pieces from the scrap awning fabric. Fold in half, right side in and long edges together. Stitch with a ½-inch seam. Press the seam open. Turn right side out. Press again so that the seam is centered in the back of the strip.

STEP 4

5 Tuck one end of the pole cup under the folded edge on the corner of the awning, opposite the edge with the button-holes. Stitch the pole cup to the corner-flap fabric only.

STEP 5

6 To assemble the frame, use the pieces cut earlier. Insert the electric tubing into one long PVC tube. Push this reinforced tube into the long casing without the buttonholes. Attach an elbow piece to each end, pushing the ends together firmly. Run a short PVC tube through each side casing and into the end of the elbow. Maneuver the fabric casing out of the way as neces-sary, and then once the join is secure, pull the fabric back into place to conceal the pipe as much as possible. Add the remain-ing pipe and elbows in the same way.

DESIGN IDEA Finish the edge of the awning with a decorative fringe. Glue the fringe in place after you've inserted the frame but before the awning is mounted. Use a permanent glue such as Fabri-Tac.

7 Lay the four-sided framed awning on a flat surface. True up the alignment, twisting the elbows as needed and tapping the ends lightly with a hammer to make sure the connections are as tight as possible. Lift the awning up to the house and guide the mounted brackets into the buttonholes. Insert a wooden pole into each pole cup. Plant the other end of the pole in a flower pot, and pile rocks around it to hold it in place. At the end of the season, take down the awning and wash it with a diluted solution of baby soap.

DESIGN IDEA Custom-sizing the awning length is easy to do. Determine the desired finished length and cut the fabric 7 inches longer. Cut the pipes that run parallel to the house 2 inches shorter than the finished length. All the other measurements and construc-tion steps remain the same, for a finished awning that extends out 36 inches from the house.

SCRAPS *of* Knowledge

SUNBRELLA FABRIC

Sunbrella fabric looks and feels like cotton, but it is actually water-repellent, fade-resistant 100 percent acrylic made especially for outdoor use. It is available in prints, stripes, and solids that would look perfect on any patio. Poppy Fab-ric in Berkeley, California, has an especially nice selection. You may also be able to buy Sunbrella fabric directly from professional awning makers. Look under "Awnings" in the Yellow Pages®.

Vinyl Table Cover with Umbrella Hole

If you like to spend time barbecuing and eating outdoors, why not make yourself a really beautiful vinyl table cover? You can pretty much choose your own look, and you might even delay the purchase of new patio furniture by sprucing up what you already have. Attractive vinylized fabrics can be found at Poppy Fabric. Another option is to have the fabric of your choice specially treated to "vinylize" the surface.

Choose a print that goes with your umbrella for this outdoor table cover.

FOR A 70-INCH ROUND
TABLE COVER, YOU'LL NEED:

- 4¼ yards vinyl fabric; allow extra to match patterns
- 1 yard soft, lightweight ⅝-inch-wide Velcro
- Six to eight decorative buttons
- Scrap of cotton fabric
- Serger
- Measuring and marking tools
- General sewing/craft supplies

185

MAKING THE TABLE COVER

1 Cut the vinyl fabric in half crosswise; then cut one piece in half lengthwise. Sew the three pieces right sides together along the long edges, the larger piece in the middle to avoid a center seam. If you need to match the pattern, cut the 70-inch-long center panel first and then match and cut the two smaller side panels to adjoin it. Finger-press the seams open.

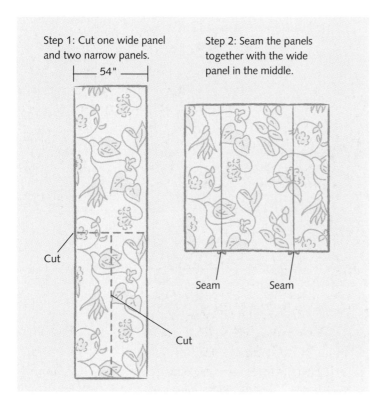

Step 1: Cut one wide panel and two narrow panels.

|— 54" —|

Cut

Cut

Step 2: Seam the panels together with the wide panel in the middle.

Seam   Seam

[**WORKROOM TIP**] If the top layer of vinyl moves ahead as you sew, switch to a roller foot for better gripping power.

2 Fold the vinyl in half, right side in, on a wooden or carpeted work surface. Fold once again into quarters. Run a pushpin through the end of a tape measure into the center point, pushing firmly into the carpet below (or use a block of wood underneath to avoid marring the floor).

STEP 2

3 Hold a fabric marker against the tape measure at the 35-inch mark, or the radius of the finished table cover. Gently swing an arc across the fabric, marking as you go. Also mark a small dot at the pushpin for the umbrella hole location.

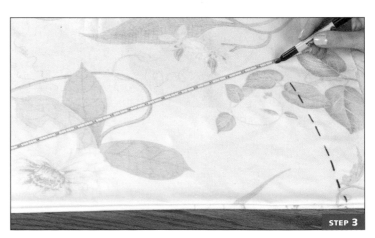

STEP 3

4 Cut along the marked line through all four layers. Open up the vinyl circle. Mark a straight line parallel to the seams from the outer edge to the center dot. Cut on this line.

5 For the umbrella opening facing, mark an 8-inch circle on cotton fabric (we used a dessert plate as a template). Serge the outer edge. Fold the facing circle in quarters. Mark and cut a small arc ¾ inch from the point.

6 To complete the umbrella hole, open the facing, fold it in half, and cut on the foldline from the outer edge to the inner cutout circle. Center the facing on the table cover, right sides together with straight cut edges matching. Machine-stitch around the inside circle ¼ inch from the edge through both layers. Clip the curved edge, and turn the facing to the wrong side. The resulting hole will be 2 inches in diameter.

ADDING THE PLACKET CLOSING

1 Cut two vinyl placket strips, each ½ inch longer than the straight open edge it will join. The extra ½ inch will be turned under at the umbrella hole edge. For the top placket, cut a 3-inch-wide strip; you may wish to match the pattern to the table cover because this placket will show. For the bottom, hidden placket, cut a 2¼-inch-wide strip.

2 Serge one long edge of the top placket, without cutting anything off. Fold the top short edge ½ inch to the wrong side. Sew a Velcro "hook" tape down the entire strip, ⅜ inch in from the serged edge, stopping ½ inch from the bottom.

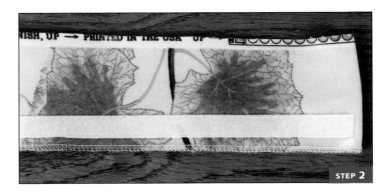

3 Place the top placket on the table cover, aligning the raw edges. Machine-stitch ⅜ inch from the edge.

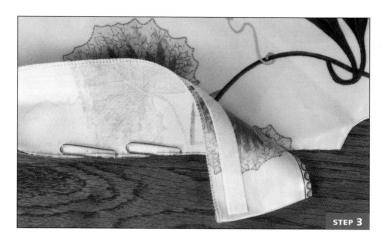

4 Fold the top placket wrong side in, so that the Velcro strip is on the underside and the visible placket is 1¼ inches wide. Topstitch ⅛ inch from the folded edge and ⅛ inch from the seam sewn in step 3. The placket will resemble the front of a man's shirt.

5 Serge both long edges of the bottom placket. Fold the top short edge ½ inch to the wrong side. Fold the entire strip in half lengthwise, and finger-press to set the crease. Place the open edge alongside the remaining long straight edge of the table cover. Enclose a scant ⅜ inch of the long straight edge with the placket, and stitch together through all layers.

6 Place the Velcro "loop" tape on the bottom placket, ⅜ inch in from the folded edge and overlapping and concealing the serged edge. Check to make sure the position corresponds to the Velcro tape on the top placket, adjust as needed, and stitch in place.

7 Serge the outer edge of the cover, pushing behind the presser foot on the serger to ease in some of the fullness. Fold the edge ½ inch to the wrong side, and topstitch in place.

STEP 7

8 Sew decorative buttons to the top placket, machine-tacking through all thicknesses.

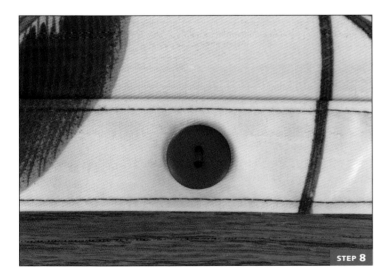

STEP 8

[WORKROOM TIP] If you do a lot of apparel sewing, you are used to using a ⅝-inch seam allowance. Home-dec sewing is different. Different seam allowances are used for different projects. Always check the project directions, and don't make assumptions.

SCRAPS of Knowledge

SEWING WITH VINYL

Vinyl has its own special handling and sewing requirements. Don't pin vinyl pieces together for sewing; instead, use paper clips, clothespins, or tape. For machine sewing, use a 70/10 H needle and a 3.5mm stitch length. It's important to avoid close, tight stitches as they will eventually weaken and tear the vinyl. Thin vinyls can be sewn with a regular presser foot, but very heavy vinyls are easier to sew with a Teflon presser foot. To prevent vinyl from sticking to the bed of the machine, use a Teflon press cloth. Cut a hole in the press cloth just large enough for the feed dogs and bobbin thread to pop through, and then tape the press cloth to the bed of the machine. To sew vinyl by hand, use a glover needle, which has a wedge-shaped point, to pierce through the dense material. You might be tempted to use upholstery thread, but don't—it requires a bigger needle and you want to avoid making large holes.

Barbecue Grill Cover

Barbecue grills are an expensive item, worth protecting from the elements, but commercially available grill covers are not always that attractive—who wants a big nondescript gray or black blob sitting on the patio? This cover is made with decorator fabric sandwiched between two layers of clear vinyl. The vinyl on the outside protects the grill from the elements, and the vinyl on the inside protects the fabric from grease stains and soot. Choose the widest-width fabric available so that you don't have to piece the large back and front panels. The worksheet will help you calculate the exact dimensions needed for your grill. If your dimensions are substantially different from our model grill, make your patterns first and take them with you when you go to buy the fabric and vinyl.

Dress up your patio with a custom-made grill cover.

TO COVER A 53-INCH BY 43-INCH BY 24-INCH GRILL, YOU'LL NEED:

- 4½ yards 54-inch-wide decorator fabric
- 9 yards 54-inch-wide clear matte-finish vinyl (available at Jo-Ann Fabrics)
- Measuring and marking tools
- General sewing/craft supplies

MAKING THE PATTERNS

1 Measure your grill using the worksheet on p. 192, and jot down your figures for A through E.

2 For the grill front/back pattern, tape sheets of newspaper together, and cut a large rectangle to your measurements A by B. Fold the paper in half, parallel to the B edges, and lay it flat with the fold at the left. Use your measurements C and D to mark dots on the top and right edges, as indicated (be sure to use ½ of C at the top). Draw a diagonal line to connect the two dots. Label the new line F, measure it, and jot it down on your worksheet. Cut on the marked line through both layers, and open out the pattern.

3 For the grill top pattern, cut a rectangle to your measurements C by E. For the grill side pattern, cut a rectangle to your measurements F plus D by E.

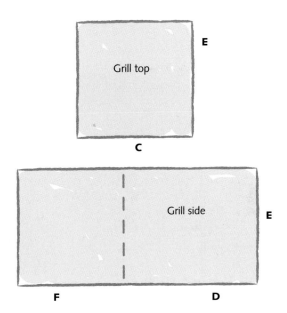

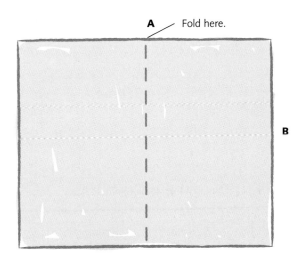

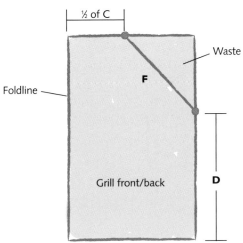

SEWING THE GRILL COVER

1 Use the three newspaper patterns to cut one front, one back, one top, and two sides from decorator fabric, adding ½ inch for the seam allowance all around. For each piece, cut two matching pieces from clear vinyl.

2 Sandwich each fabric piece between two vinyl pieces. Machine-stitch ¼ inch from the edge all around. From this point forward, treat each layered piece as a single unit.

3 Sew the top to the two sides along the E edges, right sides together, with a ½-inch seam allowance. Join the back to the top, connecting the C edges. Join the F and D edges next, clipping into the seam allowance on the side piece where it meets the angled join in the back piece. Join the front piece in the same way, first to the top and then down each side.

4 Slip the cover on the grill wrong side out. Decide on a finished length and trim off any excess evenly all around. Turn up a ½-inch hem and topstitch.

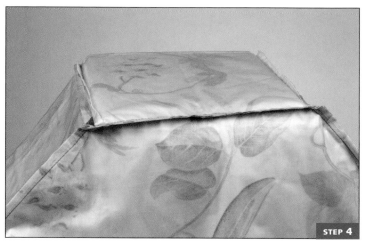

STEP 4

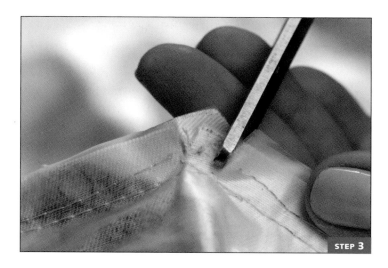

STEP 3

WORKROOM TIP Vinyl-covered fabric is water repellent but not waterproof because water can get in through the seams. Seam holes can be sealed with seam sealant to make the seams waterproof. Or you can simply store vinyl-covered items under a covered patio or awning, away from the worst weather.

BARBECUE GRILL COVER WORKSHEET

Fill in all the blanks in inches.

Overall length from end to end   (A)_____

Overall height   (B)_____

Length of the grill cover   (C)_____

Height of the side utility shelves   (D)_____

Depth at the widest part + 1" for ease (E)_____

Diagonal line (to be calculated in step 2) (F)_____

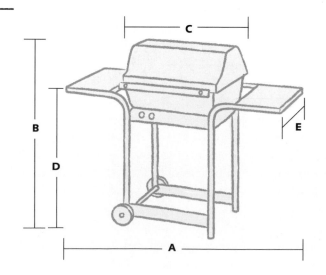

Outdoor Furniture Pads

I f your outdoor furniture pads are worn or faded or you're simply ready for something different, it's an easy task to re-cover them with new fabric. To avoid future fading, use Sunbrella or 100 percent acrylic fabric rather than natural fibers. You can cut the pieces for your new chair pad on the lengthwise or crosswise grain to take advantage of the fabric pattern. In either case, you'll probably use less than two yards of fabric. Many chair pads are a one-piece design, with Velcro hook-and-loop fasteners or ties to hold the seat and back in place. By leaving openings for the loops in the seams, you won't have to sacrifice this feature.

Replace a worn-out cushion or upgrade your favorite patio chair with a combination seat and backrest cushion.

FOR EACH NEW COVER, YOU'LL NEED:

- Original chair pad, 20 inches to 22 inches wide and 36 inches to 46 inches long
- 2 yards 54-inch-wide Sunbrella or 100 percent acrylic fabric
- 2 yards 54-inch-wide lining fabric (optional; see step 2 under Cutting the Pieces)
- Measuring and marking tools
- General sewing/craft supplies

CUTTING THE PIECES

1 Lay the Sunbrella fabric on a flat surface, right side up if the fabric pattern is a factor. Place the chair pad on top, and trace around the outer edge. Measure out 1 inch from the marked line, to allow for ½-inch ease and a ½-inch seam allowance, and mark a new outline. With the cushion still in place, mark the position of the existing ties or Velcro loops.

STEP 1

[WORKROOM TIP] On a set of chairs, a nice look (but not absolutely necessary) is to have the fabric pattern appear the same on each one. Typically, this special cutting entails waste. One way to economize is to cut all the fronts to match and all the backs to match. That way, you still have a uniform look, even if the front and back of each chair are different.

2 Cut out the chair pad top marked in step 1. Fold it in half, and retrim as needed to make the piece symmetrical. Use this piece as a template to cut the chair pad bottom. If the fabric has a loose weave or if the original cushion is dark, cut two lining pieces to match. Back each chair pad piece with its lining, and treat as one unit.

COMPLETING THE PAD

1 Place the chair pad top and bottom right sides together. Machine-stitch all around, leaving a large opening at the top of the seat back for the pad insertion and small openings for the ties. Turn right side out. Sew around the small openings by hand or machine so that the seam allowances lie flat.

2 Insert the pad through the large opening, and pull the Velcro tabs through the small openings. Close the large opening by hand.

STEP 2

Wicker Sofa Makeover

When it comes to refurbishing wicker, spray painting is the way to go. The spray reaches into all the crevices, for full and even coverage. Don't be shy when it comes to paint colors, and don't feel you have to stick with white. Old cushions can be revived with new covers sewn from Sunbrella fabric. Copy the seamlines on the original cushion to design your replacement.

A wicker sofa makeover includes a fresh coat of paint for the wicker and new covers for the cushions.

Before You Begin see **Single Welt** on p. 13.

FOR YOUR WICKER MAKEOVER, YOU'LL NEED:

- Wicker sofa with 48-inch by 27-inch seat cushion; for other sizes, adjust the yardages that follow
- 1½ yards 54-inch-wide Sunbrella fabric
- ¼ yard contrasting fabric for welt
- 2¾ yards to 4½ yards ¼-inch-diameter welt cord
- 1½ yards 1-inch-thick bonded polyester batting
- 2 large cans of gloss spray paint
- Trisodium phosphate (TSP), available at hardware stores
- Measuring and marking tools
- General sewing/craft supplies

REFURBISHING THE WICKER

1 Remove the old cushions. Wash the wicker frame with TSP, following the manufacturer's instructions, to help the paint adhere better. Let dry overnight.

2 Spray-paint the frame in the desired color, once again following the manufacturer's instructions and safety precautions. Two coats of paint give better coverage and more depth.

MAKING A NEW CUSHION

1 Examine the existing cushion cover so that you can copy its construction. For a boxing strip construction, see pp. 48–51. If your cushion has one seam centered along the edge, follow steps 2–6 below. Begin by wrapping the old cushion in bonded polyester batting, stapling or hand-basting the edges together.

[WORKROOM TIP] Whenever you use a foam insert for a cushion, wrap it in bonded poly batting, available at foam and upholstery shops. This batting will soften the edges and add dimension to the cushion.

2 Lay the Sunbrella fabric wrong side up on a flat surface. Place the cushion on top, and trace around the outer edge. (If the cushion is old and misshapen, you might want to do this step on paper and make a pattern first.) The fabric needs to extend beyond this mark to reach around the sides of the cushion. To calculate the additional allowance needed, measure the cushion depth, divide by 2, and add ½ inch. Measure out from the marked line by this amount, and mark the new outline.

3 Cut the fabric on the outside line. Fold the piece in half and retrim as needed to make it symmetrical. Use this piece as a template to cut a matching piece for the cushion bottom.

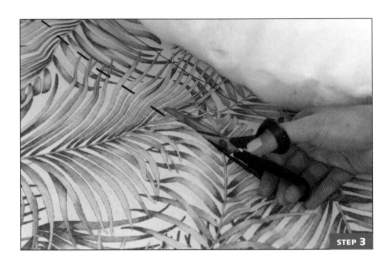

STEP 3

[WORKROOM TIP] You'll extend the life of a cushion about three years when you make it reversible. Just cut the top and bottom pieces from the same fabric, and flip the cushion over from time to time.

4 To make Turkish corners, fold each corner back on itself, right side in and raw edges matching. Sew straight down the folded corner, perpendicular to the raw edges. A stitching line 3 inches from the corner point will accommodate a 5-inch-deep cushion. A sewing line closer to the point accommodates a flatter cushion. Repeat for all eight corners. Trim off the excess bulk.

STEP 2

STEP 4

5 Make enough welt to go around the parts of the cushion that will be visible when the cushion is in place on the sofa. (If the back of a cushion is specially shaped to fit the furniture, it is not necessary to sew welt in the entire seam.) Use the ¼-inch-diameter welt cord, and cut 1⅛-inch-wide strips on the crosswise grain from the contrasting fabric. Sew the welt to the top cushion piece.

STEP 5

6 Pin the top and bottom cushion pieces right sides together. Using a zipper foot, machine-stitch over the previous stitching to join the pieces together. Leave a large opening at the back. Turn right side out, insert the cushion, and whipstitch closed.

SCRAPS of Knowledge

TURKISH CORNERS

A Turkish corner is a way to give a simple cushion cover, made from two pieces of fabric, a boxy shape. Instead of coming to a point, the fabric at each corner is folded and stitched to itself. On welted cushions, the Turkish corner stitching is done first, before the pieces are joined together. On a cushion without a welt, the pieces are sewn together and then the corners are stitched and boxed out.

RESOURCES

Here's a listing of specific fabrics and other products used to make the projects in this book. Consult the vendor listings that follow for more information.

PRODUCTS

Part 1: Kids and Pets

Baby Blanket (p. 8)
Polarfleece® from Malden Mills®

Baby Changing Pad (p. 11)
Changing pad from Simmons Juvenile Products, available at baby stores and Toys "R" Us
Vinyl-covered cotton fabric from Poppy Fabric

Child's Tepee (p. 14)
Brandywine duck fabric from Calico Corners

Child's Playhouse (p. 17)
Felt available at Jo-Ann Fabrics

Puppet Theater (p. 20)
Precut sticky letters and felt available at Jo-Ann Fabrics

Fort in a Bunk Bed (p. 22)
Air Show fabric (color: Antique) available at Calico Corners

Birdcage Cover and Seed Catcher (p. 26)
Tenwood Cage #1209 APC available at pet supply stores
Cotton fabric from The Cutting Table

Cozy Dog Bed (p. 29)
Terry cloth from The Cutting Table

Litter Box Cover (p. 31)
Cotton fabric from The Cutting Table

Part 2: Seating

Faux-Leather Hassock (p. 36)
Foam block from Creator's Foam Shop
Faux Lizard vinyl (color: Red) from Jo-Ann Fabrics

Floor Pillows (p. 38)
Burlap with oriental stamping from ABC Carpet & Home

Floor Cushions (p. 40)
Vinyl from Baer Fabrics

Bar Stool Cushion (p. 43)
Vinyl-covered cotton fabric from Poppy Fabric

Kitchen Chair Seat Covers (p. 46)
Compton fabric (color: Cocoa) from Calico Corners

Boxed Cushions for Dining Chairs (p. 48)
Foam cushion from Creator's Foam Shop
Country Life fabric (color: Black), McCheck fabric (color: Black), and Classic Ticking fabric (color: Black) from Calico Corners

Window Seats (p. 52)
Denville fabric (color: Terra Cotta) from Calico Corners

Parsons Chair Slipcover (p. 53)
Country Life fabric (color: Black), McCheck fabric (color: Black), and Classic Ticking fabric (color: Black) from Calico Corners

Buffet Silverware Holder
(p. 132)
Metallic organza from Mendel's/Far-Out
Fabrics

Elegant Table Runner (p. 135)
Silk brocade from Thai Silks

**Place Mats and Napkin
Holders** (p. 139)
Grass cloth from Poppy Fabric
Silk brocade from Thai Silks

Napkin Finishes (p. 143)
Linen fabric from Maryanne's Fabrics, etc.

Rug-Covered Coffee Table
(p. 146)
Kilim rug and LACK coffee table from
IKEA

Decorative Fireplace Screen
(p. 149)
Homasote fiberboard from Homasote Co.
Korean Figures silk crepe de chine from
Josephine's Dry Goods

Part 6: Pillows

**Television Remote Control
Pillow** (p. 154)
Quilted copper and cotton velveteen
fabrics from Stonemountain &
Daughter

Striped Ribbon Pillow (p. 156)
Ribbons from Poppy Fabric

Flange Pillow (p. 160)
Durango fabric (color: Lagoon 43) from
Calico Corners

Neck Roll (p. 162)
Silk brocade from Thai Silks

Fur Pillow with Inset (p. 166)
Faux fur imported from France by
G Street Fabrics

Picture Frame Pillow (p. 169)
Metallic silk organza from Mendel's/
Far-Out Fabrics

Jumbo Bolsters (p. 173)
Durango fabric (color: Lagoon 43) from
Calico Corners

Tufted Pillow (p. 176)
Silk dupioni from Calico Corners

Part 7: Outdoors

Awning (p. 182)
Shelby Sunbrella fabric (color: Forest)
from Calico Corners
PVC pipe from Yardbirds

**Vinyl Table Cover with
Umbrella Hole** (p. 185)
Vinyl fabric from Poppy Fabric

Barbecue Grill Cover (p. 190)
Exotica fabric (color: Sage) from Calico
Corners
Mat vinyl from Jo-Ann Fabrics

Outdoor Furniture Pads (p. 193)
Exotica fabric (color: Sage) from Calico
Corners

Wicker Sofa Makeover (p. 195)
Sunbrella fabric from Poppy Fabric

VENDORS

FABRICS

Baer Fabrics
515 E. Market St.
Louisville, KY 40202
(800) 769-7778
www.baerfabrics.com
*Home-dec, dressmaking, and car and boat
upholstery fabrics*

Banksville Designer Fabrics
115 New Canaan Ave.
Norwalk, CT 06850
(203) 846-1333
*Large selection of cashmere and cotton
velveteen, as well as other fabrics*

Calico Corners
203 Gale Lane
Kennett Square, PA 19348-1764
(800) 213-6366
www.calicocorners.com
*Huge selection of home-dec fabrics in
120 retail stores nationwide*

Carol's Zoo
992 Coral Ridge Circle
Rodeo, CA 94572
(510) 245-2020
www.carolszoo.com
*Mail-order source for faux fur; samples
available*

Custom Quilting
2832 Walnut Ave.
Tustin, CA 92780
(714) 731-7271
Machine-quilted fabrics by the yard

The Cutting Table
2499 S. Delaware Ave.
Milwaukee, WI 53207
(888) 993-2345
www.cuttingtable.com
Quilting fabric, cotton prints, and a limited but well-chosen selection of apparel fabrics; machine-quilted fabrics by the yard

G Street Fabrics
11854 Rockville Pike
Rockville, MD 20852
(301) 231-8998
www.gstreetfabrics.com
Large selection of home-dec and apparel fabrics

Jo-Ann Fabrics and Crafts
www.joann.com
Home-dec and apparel fabrics and notions; retail stores nationwide

Josephine's Dry Goods
521 S.W. 11th Ave.
Portland, OR 97205
(503) 224-4202
www.josephinesdrygoods.com
Fine apparel fabrics

Malden Mills
530 Broadway
Lawrence, MA 01841
(978) 557-3242
www.maldenmillsstore.com
Manufacturers of Polarfleece

Maryanne's Fabrics, etc.
3965 Phelan, #106
Beaumont, TX 77707
(409) 838-3965
www.maryannesfabrics.com
Nice linens, high-end dress goods

Mendel's/Far-Out Fabrics
1556 Haight St.
San Francisco, CA 94117
(415) 621-1287
www.mendels.com
Eclectic collection, including mudcloth, ikats, batiks, bright-colored fur, and costume fabrics

Poppy Fabric
5151 Broadway
Oakland, CA 94611
(800) 557-6779
Unique home-dec and vinylized fabrics; good selection of ribbons, trims, and apparel fabric; can have fabric vinylized (10 yards minimum)

Stonemountain & Daughter
2518 Shattuck Ave.
Berkeley, CA 94704
(510) 845-6106
www.stonemountainfabric.com
Good fabric resource

Thai Silks
252 State St.
Los Altos, CA 94022
(800) 722-7455
www.thaisilks.com
Biggest retail and wholesale source of silk in the United States; samples available

FOAM, PILLOW FORMS, AND COMFORTERS

Creator's Foam Shop
3510 Industrial Dr.
Santa Rosa, CA 95403
(707) 526-9774
www.foam-futon.com
All foam needs

Down Etc.
228 Townsend St.
San Francisco, CA 94107
(415) 348-0084
downetc@earthlink.net
Huge selection of pillow forms, excellent quality and prices on down and feather products; send SASE for free brochure

Garnet Hill, Inc.
231 Main St.
Franconia, NH 03580
www.garnethill.com
(800) 870-3513
Mail-order source for fine bedding; free catalog

Mulberry Silk Bedding USA
(888) 683-8882
www.silkbedding.com
Silk-filled comforters

HARDWARE AND NOTIONS

ABC Carpet & Home
888 Broadway
New York, NY 10003
(212) 473-3000
www.abchome.com
Home-dec items, good tassel and trim selection, plus a wonderful source for ideas

Clotilde, Inc.
B3000
Louisiana, MO 63353-3000
(800) 772-2891
www.clotilde.com
Mail-order notions catalog, including
zippers by the yard

Homasote Co.
P.O. Box 7240
West Trenton, NJ 08628-0240
(800) 257-9491
www.homasote.com
Manufacturers of Homasote fiberboard;
ask for a supplier in your area

IKEA
(800) 434-4532
www.ikea.com
Good resource for stylish affordable
furniture and housewares; retail stores
nationwide

Pottery Barn
(888) 779-5176
www.potterybarn.com
Unique curtain rods, brackets, and finials,
and leaf appliqués; retail stores nationwide

Sacks Industries
143 Wagner Rd.
Evans City, PA 16033
(800) 521-1635
www.sacksindustries.com
Millennium tape, double-sided and ½ inch
wide; makes a terrific substitute for the
hot-glue gun

TAP Plastics, Inc.
6475 Sierra Lane
Dublin, CA 94568
(800) 246-5055
www.tapplastics.com
Plastic and Plexiglas items

FOR FURTHER INFORMATION

American Sewing Guild
National Headquarters
9660 Hillcroft, Ste. 516
Houston TX 77096
(713) 729-3000
www.asg.org
The Guild hosts speakers and sponsors
sewing projects for the community; local
meetings open to sewers of any ability
or interest

Sewing Savvy®: Ideas for Every Room
The Needlecraft Shop®
23 Old Pecan Rd.
Big Sandy, TX 75755
(800) 449-0440
www.sewingsavvy.com
Bimonthly magazine featuring all kinds
of sewing projects; emphasis on home-
dec sewing

Sew News®
P.O. Box 56907
Boulder, CO 80322
(800) 289-6397
www.sewnews.com
Monthly magazine emphasizes apparel
sewing, but home-dec sewers will find
useful sewing machine tips

Sew What? Newsletter and Professional Drapery School
180 Buckeye Access Rd.
Swannanoa, NC 28778
(888) 993-7273
www.sewwhatnews.com
Professional drapery workroom newsletter

Threads®
The Taunton Press, Inc.
63 S. Main St., P.O. Box 5506
Newtown, CT 06470-5506
www.threadsmagazine.com
Bimonthly magazine covers creative tech-
niques and ideas for home decor, apparel,
pattern alterations, and basic sewing as
well as useful information on new products
and tools

THE AUTHORS

Sandra Betzina
95 Fifth Ave.
San Francisco, CA 94118
(415) 386-0440
www.sandrabetzina.com
Author (Fabric Savvy, Fast Fit, Power
Sewing Step-by-Step), speaker, TV person-
ality; to purchase Power Sewing products,
request a free brochure, book seminars, or
subscribe to Sandra's weekly sewing col-
umn, call or visit the website

Debbie Valentine
932 Baird Rd.
Santa Rosa, CA 95409
www.debbievalentine.com
Author, speaker; available for home-dec
sewing seminars